Praise for *Influencer*

A gem that I read in one sitting and one that I will certainly pick up time and time again.

—ANDREW GRIFFITHS
International bestselling author and global entrepreneurial speaker

Adam's nine steps are brilliant. Follow them ... you'll become a much more powerful, purposeful you. And you'll leave (and live) a great legacy as a direct result.

—PAUL DUNN
4-times TEDx Speaker, chairman of the global giving movement B1G1

The nine accelerators that Adam describes make this the most valuable social media book I have encountered.

—BRONWYN REID
Author of *Small Company, Big Business*

If you want to influence others positively you must read this book on how to do it right.

—HUNTER LEONARD
Author of *Generation Experience*, marketing strategist, speaker and philanthropist

This nine-step guide will help anyone become a LinkedIn expert, create influence and trust, and build relationships with potential clients.

—CLARE SHENG
Author of *The Suit Book: Everything You Need to Know About Wearing a Suit*

Adam's new book, *Influencer*, shares advanced strategies for building trust and credibility that are essential reading.

—VICTORIA ROSE
Author of *How to Make the Rest of Your Life the Best of Your Life*

This is a book that should not be read and put down. You should keep it on hand and treat it as a manual to refer to so you can continually increase your influence.

—STEVE BROSSMAN
Author of *Stand Up, Stand Out or Stand Aside*

Adam takes using LinkedIn to the next level and shows you concisely how to become a true influencer in your industry or niche by being known, liked and trusted. Is a must-read for anyone who uses LinkedIn.

—MICHAEL WILLIAMS

Author of *Power Profits: A Comprehensive 9-Step Framework for Reducing Electricity Costs and Boosting Profits*

In this practical, no-nonsense book, you will learn the fundamentals required to build your profile, craft your message and resonate powerfully with your ideal client.

—REBECCA COOMES

Author of the world's first SIBO cookbook, host of *The Healthy Gut* podcast

If you want to become influential in your industry, then this book is a must-read.

—KATIE MARSHALL

Author of *Chicks and Mortar: A Woman's Guide to Investing in Property*

Concise, easy to read and even easier to understand and implement. Definitely a best-in-class effort from a guy who knows the ins and outs of using LinkedIn ethically to grow your business, personal brand and influence.

—GEOFF HETHERINGTON,

The Clarity CEO, www.linkedin.com/in/geoffhetherington

The techniques and concepts are clearly laid out, and it is as simple as doing what Adam says. I can't wait to implement the advice.

—EMILY CHATHAM

Head of HR for the Y Ballarat and Y Kinders, hwww.linkedin.com/in/emily-chatham

This is the real-life practical manual on how to use LinkedIn like a pro. The strategies are easy to understand and straightforward to implement. Adam knows his stuff.

—ROBERT JAMES

Author of Amazon bestseller *Balance: How to Make Your Business and Family Life Work Together*

What an eye-opener! After posting daily on LinkedIn for the last six months, I did not get the traction I had hoped for. I now understand why, and what I need to do to get prospective clients to know me, like me and trust me so they will buy.

—ANDREA FELTON
Author of *Organise & Thrive*

Both enjoyable to read and filled with pragmatic advice.

—PAUL HENDERSON
Author of *The Chief Capability Officer* and *The Outcome Generation*

A practical, step-by-step guide for anyone looking to be seen as an influencer in their industry.

—ANN DETTORI WILSON
Author of The *Entrepreneurs' Guide to Self-Publishing*

This book combines step-by-step instructions with tips and research and is crystal clear on how to start or to enhance your profile on LinkedIn.

—CAROLYN S DEAN
Author of *Fully Booked: Dental Marketing Secrets for a Full Appointment Book*

The game-changing book every information-hungry-yet-time-poor entrepreneur needs to read.

—NATALIE STEVENS
Author of Amazon #1 bestseller *Building Home*

This book is the blueprint on how to become more influential in order to make a bigger impact in your industry.

—TRACY ANGWIN
Australian Payroll Association

If you want to be in the top percentage of people creating impact and able to stand out in a crowded market space, then this book is a must-read.

MELISSA MCCONAGHY
Author of *The New Parkinson's Treatment: Exercise is Medicine*

Adam has cracked a vital marketing code that once had me so confused. Full of practical, personal and proven tips, it shares a simple strategy for success that just makes sense, even to rookies like me.

—SONJA WALKER

Author of bestseller *School Ready: A Practical and Supportive Guide for Parents With Sensitive Kids*

The
9 step guide
to becoming
highly influential
in any industry

Influencer

Adam Houlahan

AUTHOR OF AMAZON BESTSELLERS

Social Media Secret Sauce & The LinkedIn Playbook

First published 2018
This edition published 2023 by The Dubai Trust

Produced by Indie Experts P/L, Australasia
indieexperts.com.au

Copyright © Adam Houlahan 2023

Cover design by Daniela Catucci @ Catucci Design
Edited by Anne-Marie Tripp
Internal design by Indie Experts
Typeset in 11.5/17 pt Minion Pro by Post Pre-press Group, Brisbane

 A catalogue record for this book is available from the National Library of Australia

ISBN 978-0-6453538-2-2 (paperback)
ISBN 978-0-6453538-3-9 (epub)

This book is dedicated to one of my longest-serving mentors and business advisors, my good mate, Raymond P. Wood. As an author and speaker, you'd think words would come easily to me. They fail me right now in expressing my love and respect for this pillar of the human race. My heartfelt gratitude to him for the positive influence he has been. Without his guidance and—most importantly—friendship, I would not be at this point in my life.

Thank you, you bloody legend!

Contents

Updated for 2023

Before I started working on this book back in 2014, I talked with my writing mentor Andrew Griffiths as he critiqued my first book, *Social Media Secret Sauce*. His wise words were: 'Adam, this is a great book. The challenge you'll face in writing books on social media is the constant change that occurs. If you are going to go down this path, you'll need to be prepared to release regular updates.'

As time has gone by, and we're now updating *Influencer* for the third time in six years, I'm struck once again by how right he was about that.

While the 2021 edition captured a lot of relevant updates to the rapidly-moving social media industry, the changes in this new edition for 2023 are a solid reflection of just how much social media and online business has evolved, including the significant changes to how we collectively meet, engage, and transact business online since the onset of the global COVID-19 pandemic. Other changes reflect the changing way we, as consumers of content, prefer to access and digest our information.

LinkedIn has continued its relentless march forward in being the undisputed leader of business-related social platforms. Recent changes on the platform confirm that LinkedIn is leading the way once more in innovation, which has become even more relevant and necessary, with many features now actively helping members to conduct and grow their business, as opposed to simply connecting and marketing their expertise. Some of the special features, such as a wider use of audio, event management, and live rooms has revolutionised some people's functionality in business overall. As you'll see, these new tools and features are free for members, and do not require premium membership. This is a positive way that LinkedIn has continued to embrace and support the changing requirements of a more flexible and globally-focused business environment.

With this update, I have removed any sections that have either become redundant or no longer best practice, and added updated suggestions based on the results we have been achieving with our clients all over the world. None of what you will read ahead is theory; everything is based on the real world, with tried and proven strategies developed by myself and our amazing team at Prominence Global.

In the 2021 edition, I added two new chapters: 'The Pyramid of Players' and 'Know-How *vs* No-How'. 'The Pyramid of Players' is my best thinking and the process upon which all of our programs are built and taught, so it made sense to include it here for you. 'Know-How *vs* No-How' remains the fundamental principle upon which your entire content strategy needs to be built, so please do read this chapter more than once. **If you can embrace this concept, it will change your content strategy forevermore.**

This new edition, updated for 2023, features a particularly valuable addition about Company Pages and why these are so necessary if you really want to step up into being an influencer of value. Along with a clear explanation of how to create your Company Page and utilise the many features of this area, we've also made it easy for you to see the benefits of these powerful features in our case study profiles, as several of them express the value they discovered in having a solid Company Page.

All of the case studies included in this book will give you great insights into the outcomes you should be striving for and what is truly important in the journey to influence.

I suggest that this is not the type of book you'll read once, and then put on your bookshelf as testament to your growing list of books read. It's designed to be a reference source and workbook of sorts.

I highly recommend you read a section then implement it straight away. Binge-read the entire book if you choose to, then come back and start again, implementing section by section. Via emails or in person at events around the world, I have spoken to thousands of people who have read the previous editions of this book. The underlying theme of those conversations was always that people achieved the best results from doing just that: implementing step by step.

Adam

The Power and Necessity of Influence

Influence: The ability to be a compelling force or to produce effects on the actions, behaviour, and opinions of others.

Like it or not, we live in a digital world where instant fame and its financial rewards can be just one viral post away. Almost daily, we hear stories of people becoming overnight millionaires simply by winning a lottery of some description, yet few of us personally know anyone who has come into such good fortune.

Equally, we could search online right now and find examples of people who have been in the right place at the right time to capture on camera their pets, children or friends doing something a little out of the ordinary, funny, or dangerous that the online global community has found worthy of interaction, and the content has gone viral.

This is the influence of our social platforms at work. Instant (though usually fleeting) fame and financial rewards have been achieved with seemingly little or no effort. Yet like those lottery winners, very few of us personally know any of these overnight 'instafamous' people.

To some degree, influence can also be gained by having a healthy bank account, or a position of authority. These versions of influence can be maintained with little or no respect for the individual. We might be envious of the wealth or status of these people, but more than likely, we speak of them in negative vernacular at every opportunity.

Let me share with you what this book is *not* about.

If you're looking for the secrets to creating instant fame and fortune, you won't find them here. This book is not about online hacks, and it does not contain tips on viral posts to promote on various social platforms, leading to instant stardom and wealth. Equally, you'll find nothing about gaining a position above others, enabling you to force your will upon them, or about buying agreement for your opinions or desires.

This book is written for those who choose to use their knowledge and expertise as forces for good, and by doing so earn the respect of their peers and those they have the privilege to serve and impact in profound ways.

It's for those who wish to affect change in a positive manner, through self-improvement, which means they deliver their value to the world with a sense of commitment and purpose.

If this sounds like you, then read on. You will discover that there are three key requirements, or pillars, that create the recipe for (and the hitherto secret ingredients of) influence:

1. Getting known
2. Being liked
3. Being trusted

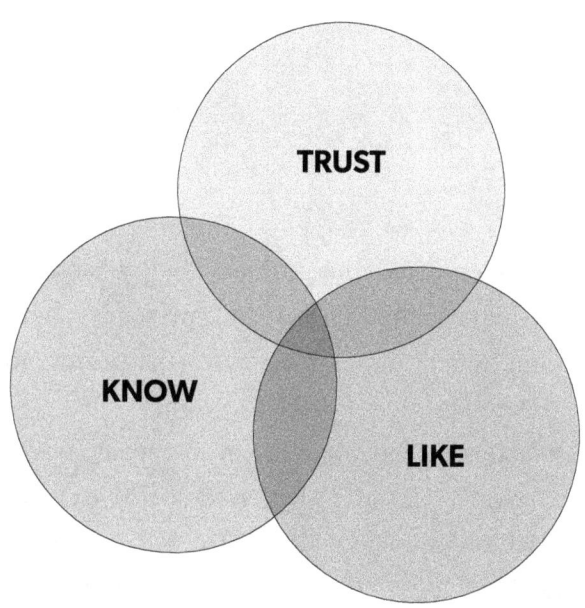

Each of these three *pillars* have three *accelerators*. Understanding the role of these pillars, and their accompanying accelerators, **is the key to creating your action plan** so that you can also appear to become an overnight success. Let's begin by identifying those nine accelerators and why they matter.

GETTING KNOWN

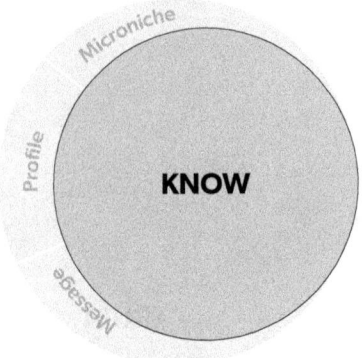

1. **Your online profile.** Your profile is your greatest asset, yet it is fragile. Years of building a credible presence can be destroyed with one wrong move. We'll cover the process for creating and protecting yours for years to come.

2. **Microniches.** When you attempt to appeal to everyone, you attract no one; in today's hyper-competitive environment it's essential to dominate a *microniche*. We dive deeply into this concept and look at how you can discover yours, and why this accelerator could change the way you market yourself forevermore.

3. **Your message.** Clarity around the value you deliver and what it is you stand for is paramount in creating influence. I'll share with you a simple framework to use to get very clear about who you are, what you do and for whom you do it.

BEING LIKED

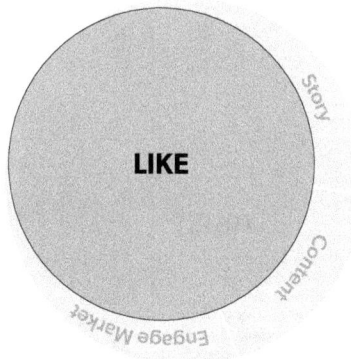

1. **Stories.** We're in a story-telling age, and the most important story of all is yours, closely followed by that of your clients, and the product or service you deliver. How you tell these stories is critical to becoming influential.

2. **Engagement.** While the world is focused on the metrics of people who engage with our content, true influencers measure their own engagement in a very different way. I will share with you the process of measuring yours and understanding why this is important.

3. **The power of content.** There are five types of content to focus on, and the mix is important. Of the nine accelerators, the content you create and the people you create it for will build your pathway to success.

BEING TRUSTED

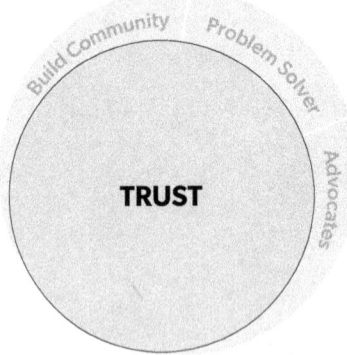

1. **Community.** Influencers polarise their audience and embrace the people who believe what they believe. It's not your task to change the opinion of anyone who has one and chooses to express it; your role is to find your tribe and nurture them in order to deliver your greatest value to those willing to accept your point of view.

2. **Problem solving.** When problems are solved, you swim in rivers of gold. The majority of people online are there to be entertained or to find a solution to a problem; once you focus on problem solving, you become the go-to person in your industry: the person of influence. Yet this is also where the majority of content creators get it wrong. I will share with you the fundamental shift you need to make that will dramatically increase your conversion rates.

3. **Creating advocates.** You will have achieved influence when everyone else says so. The internet is awash with self-proclaimed experts or gurus on every topic known to man.

Real influence is measured by the opinion of others who openly share your message and their opinion of you at every opportunity.

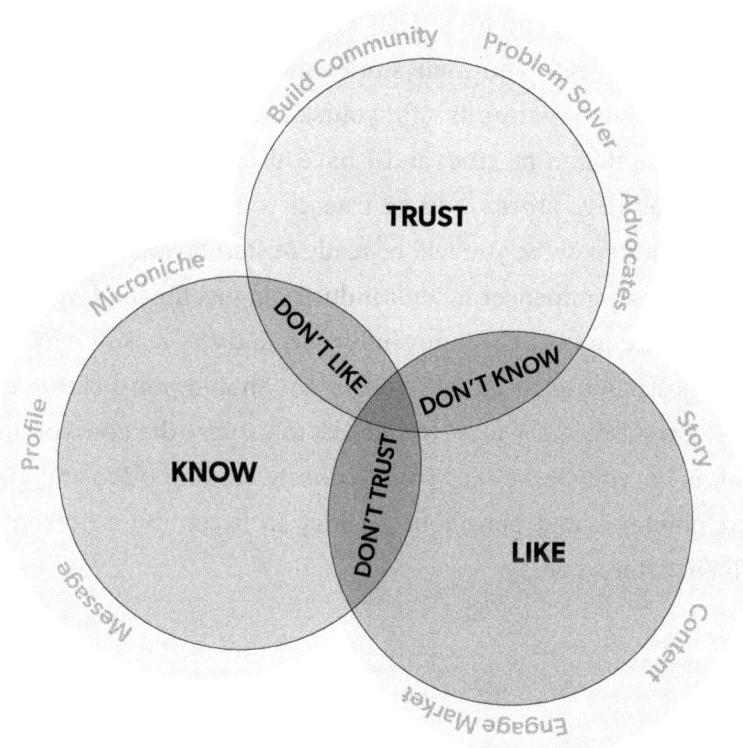

On more than a few occasions in interviews or during keynote presentations I've been asked *that* question: 'What is your secret to becoming an overnight success?' My answer is always, 'I don't know. I've never become that, or met anyone who has.' I have, however, met many people who, through persistence, focus and working to a plan, have been able to appear as though they transitioned from obscurity to highly influential overnight.

Throughout this book, you will find case studies of real people who have used this exact process to make an incredible difference to their businesses and lives. They are everyday people from many different industries, and their stories showcase how you can also create amazing opportunities for yourself and your business.

I believe this to be true, and I have also coached hundreds of people who have *proven* it to be true. If you follow the principles outlined in *Influencer*, you will be ready to start creating a powerful position as an influencer in your industry in just ninety days.

These are my beliefs about influence, and the reason why you might just choose to elevate your own. Should you believe as I believe, or at the very least would like to explore the concept, this book is for you. Settle into your favourite reading place and grab your notebook and pen. Your journey to becoming a person of influence starts here.

CHAPTER 1

My Story

The first step in writing a new book is always months of research. It seems that with each new book I write, I spend more and more time in this phase, and *Influencer* was no exception—for the original version and both of the updated editions.

For me, research is about more than just the topic. I'm always interested in asking what type of book my readers really want to read. When I asked this question of tens of thousands of people, I was surprised by their responses; not only the feedback on the question itself but also by the common thread running through the extra information shared.

One of the responses I received was this: *Adam, I don't mind what book you write next, but what I would really love to read is your story, your journey, that brought you to where you are and what you do today.*

I was a little shocked at first; not at the thought of including such personal information in my next book, but that anyone would be interested in reading about me. After more deliberation and questions about this, I decided to share the background to my work, this book, and why I'm passionate about sharing my knowledge with you.

My journey to this point has included being self-employed since the age of twenty-four, several successful business partnerships, travel that opened me up to a bigger world and picture of the future I wanted for myself, and enriched learning and study of what has interested me along the way. Finally, I was turned on to the extraordinary power and potential of LinkedIn.

But let's start at the beginning.

I opened my first business on the Gold Coast in Queensland, Australia, having decided to turn my hobby of skiing into a business. My water- and snow-ski shop was started up with two good mates, Ray Wood and Stuart Harker. These two fine gents possessed greater wisdom than I, and I can say without a doubt that without their collective wisdom, I would almost certainly have joined the huge percentage of small-business start-ups that fail within two years. However, survive and grow we did.

They were both silent partners, and so did not hold active roles within the business on a daily basis. The plain truth is that I had needed their wisdom, business experience and cash in equal measure to get started in my first business venture; that early experience taught me the value of mentors and coaches, and I have had both ever since.

Over the years both Stuart and Ray sold their shares back to me and went on to other successful ventures and careers. I met Ray through Stuart, and I want to acknowledge that Ray Wood has been one of the most important people to have guided my journey, starting with the first day that we met to discuss becoming business partners and going right through until today. He remains one of my closest friends, and has been a foundational rock in every facet of my life, personally, and also as a guiding light throughout my career. Ray has been there for me through some of the darkest days of my life, and has celebrated every win with me, which is why I have dedicated this book to him.

My world opens up

It was through this first business that I also found my passion for travel, and during the fourteen years that the business was a part of my life, I travelled to Hong Kong, New Zealand, Japan, the United States and Canada. In particular, I went to the United States many times, often twice a year, to visit suppliers and attend trade shows.

Since those early days I have had the good fortune to travel overseas on more than eighty occasions and have so far visited twenty-seven countries in this amazing world we live in.

During one of my trips to Orlando, Florida, I ran into former Australian world champion slalom skier Brett Thurley, who I knew from the skiing industry back home. At the time, Brett was vice president of the Texas-based company Tige Boats and they were looking for an Australian distributor for their incredible brand of luxury wakeboard boats. Over a couple of dinners in Orlando with

Brett and Tige's founder, Charlie Pigeon, Tige Boats Australia was born.[1]

By this time my water- and snow-ski retail business had grown, and we had formed a partnership with Chris Grady of the Brisbane-based business Waterskiers Connection. Chris and I purchased a third store in Brisbane: Waterskiers World. Over time, I was able to become less focused on the retail businesses because Chris was doing such a great job running them, so I could devote more time to Tige.

Eventually the time came for me to exit the retail stores[2] and Tige became the central part of my business life for a number of years until 2004, which was to prove a pivotal year. During 2004, my first wife and I separated, and in 2005, I sold Tige to my partners during our divorce, although I remained for a few more years as its CEO. This proved to be a bittersweet time, with so many changes happening in my life. The bitter part of this is best left untold, but the sweet part was marrying Julie, my beautiful wife now for the last sixteen years. Julie and I decided to have a child a couple of years after we married, and when Julie was pregnant with our daughter Tyla, I left Tige.

I was about to become a dad once again. I have a son and daughter from my first marriage, Julie has two sons from her first marriage, and Tyla would make five children between us. At this

---

1 www.tige.com
2 Two of these stores were sold to new owners, and Chris retained Waterskiers Connection for many years and until recently decided to sell up and move to the Gold Coast where my wife Julie and I also live. Chris and I remain good friends to this day.

point I had no business, no job and no idea what was next. We were in a good position to simply focus on the impending arrival of Tyla and let the universe guide my next career move. And guide us in mysterious ways it did.

In 2010, I met Colin and Narelle Chenery and Alf Orpen, who owned the company Organic and Natural Enterprise Group (ONEgroup). I quickly fell in love with this company and its mission to produce some of the world's best certified-organic products and maintain a focus on sustainability. I was invited to join them and be a part of ONEgroup where I stayed for more than six years.

Discovering social media

It was during my time at ONEgroup that my passion for social media was born. The first of my two roles with the company was as retail manager before I went on to become general manager. As retail manager, I researched companies around the world that operated in a similar way to ONEgroup in the production of its skincare lines. I was interested in finding out what was the differentiator between companies that experienced rapid growth and those that did not. It turned out these rapid-growth companies were early adopters of social media, which convinced me that this social media thing was here to stay, and that businesses of the future would need to master this relatively new phenomenon.

I should disclose that at this time, 2010, I knew absolutely nothing about social media. I had a Facebook account like most people, and probably looked at it once a week. Although I didn't know it at the time, this 'ah-ha' moment planted the seed that directed my life's journey and where I would go in the future.

My interest in social media started out as a focus on how it would help ONEgroup deliver the message of the importance of organic products and sustainability to the world. It quickly became my passion; Julie called it an obsession and she was probably correct, as she almost always is.

In my spare time, I did extensive research on social media. When I became the general manager, I was able to reach out to some of the world's leading people in this area at the time, and leverage their knowledge and skills to further my own understanding. This led to me consulting for and owning a share in a social media business for a period of time.

Over time I became most interested in LinkedIn. It just made sense to me personally as my background was very much business focused, and getting to understand LinkedIn and how to best utilise it became my sub-passion. This passion for LinkedIn continues to this day.

I had also started to develop a small consulting business at this time. I had a few clients and helped them mainly with their use of social media, but it was not much more than a hobby and gave me a little extra income.

In my opinion, this is where the story gets interesting, but you can be the judge.

LinkedIn changes everything

In 2013, I received a direct message on LinkedIn from someone who wanted to connect with me. I looked into his profile, and he seemed quite an interesting guy so I accepted his connection request. He was a business-development manager for a company based in Melbourne, but with offices in the United Kingdom, Singapore and the United States. We sent a few messages back and forth—just basic get-to-know-you stuff—and a few weeks later, he suggested that I come to a dinner so we could meet face-to-face. I could also meet the co-founder of his company, which was putting on the dinner for business owners in Brisbane, Australia.

Brisbane is an hour's drive north of where I live, and I recall thinking twice about accepting the offer. Yet, accept I did.

On the day of the dinner, I had a long, challenging day at ONEgroup and in the afternoon I made the decision to give the dinner a miss. I jumped in my car to head home that evening. I came to the intersection at the end of the street, where I usually turned right towards home. If I turned left, I would connect with the M1 north to Brisbane.

The traffic on this evening was unusually heavy, and as I sat waiting at the intersection, I had what I now refer to as my 'sliding-doors moment'. Turn right and go home to Julie and the children, or turn left and go to the dinner. I recall agonising over that decision. I had said I would attend, and I knew I should make the effort. The car basically steered itself as I turned left and headed for Brisbane. That decision would radically change the course of my life forever.

At the dinner, the speaker was Glen Carlson, co-founder of the business that, at that time, was called Key Person of Influence and today is known as Dent.[3] Glen's style was relaxed and his message resonated with me a great deal. We sat together for a time after the meal was served and got to know each other a little better. I agreed to come along to a one-day event he was running at the Brisbane Convention Centre a couple of weeks later.

The event turned out to be one of the best I had ever attended. I caught up with Glen again that day, and we chatted some more about what I was doing in the social media consulting space. The next step for me was to go to a more in-depth meeting about the program Key Person of Influence (KPI), a forty-week commitment and, at the time, an investment of a little over $10,000. I was not going to make such a decision without speaking to Julie, and I headed home after a well-spent Saturday in Brisbane.

At this point, life got in the way as it tends to do, and I missed the next meeting.

Some weeks later, Glen called me out of the blue and said he was coming back to Brisbane and had some time for breakfast before returning to Melbourne. It was at this meeting that I decided to join the program.

I was now juggling a full-time role at ONEgroup, a small consulting business, a forty-week training program, and a family, which included a toddler who didn't seem to understand the concept of sleep. On the upside, I soon discovered a new waking time each day of four am, which enabled me to get everything done.

---

3 www.dent.global

Part of the KPI process was for each individual to write a book about their area of expertise; I amended my new waking time to three am, with some extra work on weekends and every evening, and I embraced a new passion for writing.

My first book, *Social Media Secret Sauce*, was launched in 2014. The KPI program was a real game changer for me, as was the publication of my first book. These two events set me on the path I am on today and most likely will be on for the rest of my life. However, this pathway has more to add to the story; it set me on a trajectory to meet the two people who would become the most significant influencers in my life—apart from Ray Wood and the amazing Julie Houlahan.

Mentors and influencers

Dr David Dugan[4] was one of the KPI mentors, and I learned a great deal from him. We became close friends throughout the course of the forty-week program. David also runs Abundance Global, which I am still a member of to this day. After the KPI program had finished, David invited me to be a speaker at one of his events to talk about my book, and social media in general.

Over time, David and I did more and more together, and in 2016 we decided to launch Web Traffic That Works (which has since been renamed Prominence Global[5]) as a joint enterprise. David remains my business partner, coach and close friend to this day; he was, and

---

4 www.daviddugan.com
5 www.prominence.global

still is, an integral part of the success that our company has achieved on a global scale.

David also had a hand in one of the world's most respected mentors becoming my mentor and close friend. When David asked me to speak at his event, he said, 'Adam, there's someone coming to this event I want you to meet. Paul Dunn will be the other keynote speaker apart from you, so you'll get to spend some time with him over the two days.'

Paul Dunn, as I have mentioned, is an incredible mentor to many well-known names in the entrepreneur circles of Australia, the UK, the US and New Zealand; a list that includes David Dugan, Glen Carlson and Glen's business partner Daniel Priestley, and many more. Paul is also a philanthropist and chairman of the global giving movement B1G1.[6]

To say that Paul and I had an instant rapport at David's event would be to understate those two days, and the impact Paul has had on my life since. In a phone call to Paul when he returned home to Singapore a week later, I described our meeting as being as impactful as seeing the births of my children, and it was.

Paul's guidance in my career and life journey since that day has been profound. One of his greatest impacts had been to open my eyes to the ability of businesses of any size to participate in philanthropic projects that make this world a better place. One of my greatest joys and proudest achievements is to have impacted the lives of over nine million people through B1G1 and Prominence Global.[7]

---

6 www.B1G1.com
7 You can see more on this at www.prominence.global/impact.

These days I live on the beautiful Gold Coast of Australia with my wife Julie, and spend my time speaking at business events both online and live. My presentations are almost always about LinkedIn and the ways to leverage this platform from a personal and business perspective. Four of our children have grown up and left school and are now on their own life journeys. Tyla is the exception; she's more than halfway through her school years. I really can't imagine right now what the future world will be like when she ends that journey and commences the next in five years from now.

You will also find me regularly working from a laptop in one of the Gold Coast's many coffee shops, or on a park bench beside one of our many beautiful beaches.[8] Our company, Prominence Global, has a professional team of superstars across the world who, like me, live a laptop lifestyle, and work with incredible business leaders across the globe every day.

This is my story and my journey. I hope you enjoyed reading about it as much as I enjoyed sharing it with you, but now let's get into the true purpose of this book.

---

8 www.destinationgoldcoast.com

CHAPTER 2

The Value of Being Influential

'The key to successful leadership today is about influence, not authority.' —**Ken Blanchard**

Why would you want to be influential? This is a question I have now asked of over 1,000 entrepreneurs, and understandably I hear a wide range of answers. There is, however, a common theme that stands out.

Bearing in mind that most people are referring to the way they succeed with their online marketing, personal branding, and of course their LinkedIn presence, the responses almost always revolve around the ease with which they can create traction to fill webinars, live events and membership programs, and get face-to-face meetings with potential clients. The premise being that if you're seen to be highly knowledgeable in your industry and in demand, people are more likely to want to hear what you have to say.

The agglomeration of these answers can be summed up in two words: *Peerless Positioning.*

I agree with this premise, and with the concept that influence equals Peerless Positioning, provided of course that the product or service is world class, and the way both are presented is clearly articulated and valued by whomever they are being presented to.

Influence is best achieved through creating your personal brand, and there are a multitude of good books, courses and people willing to help you create yours. Everyone—your team, your clients and potential clients, and especially the media if you're seeking heavy exposure—will be swayed in their opinion of you through your personal brand. LinkedIn is one of the best platforms to develop that brand in two very important ways.

Firstly, LinkedIn gives you the opportunity to showcase yourself through imagery, i.e., your profile image, background image, and any other images or video you attach to your profile. Secondly, you can outline in words through the About and Experience sections everything about you, including what you stand for.

It's my belief, and also my experience, that the written content on LinkedIn is what will give you the greatest opportunity to create your brand. As mentioned, it can be done in the About and Experience sections, but equally important is the ability to create and share content or express opinions on the platform. This is what will set you on your journey to influence, but so few people get it right and let me share why.

At the time of writing, there are four critical numbers that tell the story:

1. 850 million
2. 3.5 million

3. 200,000

4. 0.02 percent

The first number is a rough estimate of how many people are currently on LinkedIn, which is around 850 million and this number is still growing by two additional profiles every second of every day of every week of every year. Taken in isolation, that might seem like a huge pool of people (and it is), so how on earth can you stand out in such a crowd?

The second number, 3.5 million, is again a rough estimate, and it relates to how many of those 850 million profiles are *content creators*. This means that they create original content on a regular basis and post to either the publisher platform or as status posts, and it includes creators of video content. I will cover this in more depth in later chapters, but for now take my word for it that influence that comes from your content creation is the number one of all nine accelerators.

The third number, 200,000, is a rough guide as to how many of these creators are generating the type of content that engenders influence.

I put it to you that if you know how to create the right type of content, and do this consistently, you have what I know to be an unprecedented opportunity to become one of the very few people—in fact, one of just 0.02 percent of all people on LinkedIn—with the ability to generate real influence and Peerless Positioning. The good news is that by the time you finish reading this book that is exactly what you will have, plus the other eight influence accelerators.

Combined, these influence accelerators will form the roadmap for creating your pathway in the next ninety days to becoming an influencer for your business and in your industry.

I want to make it very clear at this point that I am not talking about what is termed 'influencer marketing'. Let me explain the difference between this and the *why*, and how you can become an influencer yourself.

Influencer marketing

You only have to do a search using the term 'influencer marketing' to find millions of articles on the subject, and this alone should tell you it's one of the hot topics or buzz phrases of our day. If you've read my book, *The LinkedIn Playbook*, you would know I made a similar distinction between social selling and social serving.

Influencer marketing is the practice whereby you leverage someone else's influence by engaging them to represent your brand. It is these people that your ideal clients or customers perceive as being credible—more so than you or your brand and business. The opinions and often buying habits of others are swayed by these people's endorsement of you. Influencer marketing is big business: by 2022, it was estimated to be worth US$16.5 billion and the number of influencer marketing companies worldwide had increased by a staggering 26 percent over the previous year, up to 18,900 companies.

It is a niche area, and often people you have never heard of and are unlikely to ever hear of, many of whom are school age, are at the low end of this practice, receiving free products, holidays, accommodation and so on, up to the high end of the spectrum, which represents millions of dollars to align with brands. I personally endorse a number of companies as an influencer for their brands under this practice.

Again, let me be very clear: I have no issue whatsoever with influencer marketing, given that I participate in this practice regularly. But influencer marketing is very different to being an influencer within your industry.

Becoming an influencer

I won't be showing you a pathway to becoming an influencer in the above sense. I will be showing you a proven method that I have used myself, and many of the people I coach have used, to become influential within a microniche.

A microniche is centred on your personal experience or the business you use to generate revenue month after month, year after year. It's designed to place you firmly in the driver's seat, in control of your ability to generate income for yourself and your family. You set the price, you choose with whom you work, and you are seen as the person of influence within your industry.

That industry could range from local to global. The underlying premise is not to be using the term 'influencer', which is what many people are doing online these days, whether or not they actually are influencers. True influence is obtained when your market refers to you as such, not when you add this term to your website, LinkedIn profile or marketing copy.

Does this mean you cannot or should not take up or seek opportunities within the influencer-marketing juggernaut? It's entirely up to you to decide, if and when those opportunities present themselves. My methodology is about something more predictable and controllable than influencer marketing.

Is becoming an influencer in this sense the only way to market your business in the coming years? Of course not, and nor will it suit everyone. It could potentially be a great option for you, and you may still decide it's not your cup of tea. But at the very least you will have the information required to make the decision to jump right into the process, or explore different opportunities more suited to your choice of marketing.

Why might you choose to become an influencer in this way? I believe there currently exists a rare opportunity to do something very few people in the world are doing exceptionally well, which is to create new opportunities to market themselves and/or their businesses in a powerful way.

CHAPTER 3

The Three Pillars of Influence

'I hold that a strongly marked personality can influence
descendants for generations.' —**Beatrix Potter**

There is a very simple framework to becoming influential, and it consists of three pillars and nine accelerators. Let's start with those three pillars, which form the basis of the nine accelerators:

Pillar #1: Know
Pillar #2: Like
Pillar #3: Trust

In order for you to become influential, people have to undertake a journey with you. They first need to discover you: this is the *know*. Once they have discovered you, they then have to decide what they think of you and, more importantly, how they feel about what you stand for: this is the *like*. And finally, they have to have confidence in who you are, what you have to say, what you stand for, and your expertise: this is the *trust*.

How you create your influencer strategy has to, in the simplest of goals, take your tribe on this journey of discovery.

Before people can get to know you, they first need to be able to find you, and this is where LinkedIn will become your best friend. You could spend many thousands of dollars on a personal website and then tens of thousands more in search engine optimisation (SEO) strategies and/or Google Ads (formerly AdWords) campaigns every year to make sure your website is found in searches—or you could, at no cost, set up an exceptional profile on LinkedIn.

I've already shared with you how many profiles are on LinkedIn at the time of writing (850 million) and how this number is growing at a phenomenal pace. But remember that only 0.02 percent of LinkedIn profiles could be considered highly influential, and yet every day I still see so many profiles that are underwhelming and damaging to these people's personal brand. The very first step in this journey is to make sure you have an exceptional profile. This will be the first impression people have of you, and you have just a few seconds to make it great.

If you have a copy of *The LinkedIn Playbook*, you already have a comprehensive guide on how to do this to a high standard. If you have a copy but haven't yet updated your profile using the *Playbook* methodology, I suggest you stop at the end of this chapter and get it done before moving on.

If you don't have a copy of *The LinkedIn Playbook* you can buy the paperback or Kindle versions on Amazon.

Pillar #1: Know

At this point I will assume that you have an amazing profile on LinkedIn, or that you will have very soon. It's important that you do have because this is where you will give people the opportunity to get to know you.

Background image. There is one thing that will have great impact and give people the first opportunity to know who you are. It will do more than anything else to capture people's attention, and this is your background image. This is one of the most underused yet most visible representations of you.

We tend to absorb information in at least one of three ways: visual images, written content, or video. To use myself as an example, I'm not able to process video content very well; you only have to ask my wife Julie to know I cannot read a map to save my life; equally, infographics make little sense for me. However, give me a step-by-step written process and I will follow it to the letter.

Make sure that people can experience all three; they will undoubtedly prefer one to another and you want to cover all bases. So make sure you have a great background image.

Written content. You have just 2,600 characters of text for your Summary section and your position descriptions in your Experience section allow you 2,000, so use them wisely to present your written roadmap to those whose preference is to absorb information through the written word.

Video. Invest in a really good video that gives some context for who you are. I would suggest keeping it under two minutes.

Keywords. If you have followed the *Playbook* methodology, you will have included strong keywords that help LinkedIn show your profile to people during their searches. This will be one of your greatest friends with regard to free and targeted visibility on your profile, and it will be your first step in allowing people to get to know you. The next step is by your connection strategy, and the last step is through your amazing content.

Pillar #2: Like

Ask yourself this question: When was the last time you purchased anything from someone you really dislike?

Make yourself the first choice. There are times when we have no choice but to deal with people we dislike. As an example, in my previous home we had no option when it came to service providers for our home phone connection. No matter how much I disliked this service provider (and I really did), if I wanted a home phone service, I had to use them.

In most cases, however, we have a degree of choice, and likewise it's almost a certainty that you will not be the only option available in the service you provide. But even if you are, the long-term viability of your business will always be better if your clients love you instead of seeing you as the only option. I'm certain that if they do like you, it will have some bearing on their purchasing decisions in the future.

Post online content wisely. I'm not suggesting that you need to undergo a personality transplant or change yourself in significant ways. But I am suggesting that you are careful about what you post on LinkedIn (this won't be an issue if you follow the content guide I will share in coming chapters). Of equal or perhaps more importance, you should also be careful about what you post on any other social media profiles.

I personally know people who have lost job and client opportunities due to some less than savoury posts on platforms like Facebook, Instagram, Snapchat, and so on. You may recall that in 2018, Roseanne Barr's new TV sitcom was axed after an 'ill-worded' post caused condemnation all the way to the White House, and internationally.

I can assure you that once someone has decided to explore the option of engaging your services, they are highly likely to do a search on you and see what turns up.

If you haven't done a search on your own name recently, do it now. Open your favourite browser, type in your name and see what comes up online about you. Most likely you will find that any social media profiles you have will be readily available and anyone can access them from these search results.

You could choose to set some of your social media profiles to private, and that would help somewhat if you decide it would not be to your advantage for people to see certain posts, but it will be a lot easier to become influential if you're not plagued by any untoward online content.

What I really mean by 'like' in this context is that people like the content you share online. This is as simple as ensuring that your content strategy is designed to appeal to a microniche of the market. The word 'like' also means that people find you open and engaging, and when you do share content, they feel inclined to comment or share on your behalf.

Find your tribe. The best influencers engage with their tribe and are respectful of the value and privilege involved in having people choose to express their opinions or praise of you. But choose your tribe wisely; you don't need everyone to like you, and there is real value in polarising your tribe.

Pillar #3: Trust

'Trust is the glue of life. It's the most essential ingredient
in effective communication. It's the foundational principle
that holds all relationships.' —**Stephen Covey**

When was the last time you purchased anything from someone you really didn't trust? There were probably near zero times you were okay with doing that.

Major brands spend millions of advertising dollars in the pursuit of building trust in their brands, or in rebuilding it when they lose it. And while you don't need to spend a great deal on this, you do need to be perceived as trustworthy if your influence is going to be a revenue driver for you.

Stephen Covey wrote an exceptional book on trust called *The Speed of Trust*, and it has some great quotes. One of my personal favourites is: 'Over time, I have come to this simple definition of leadership: Leadership is getting results in a way that inspires trust.'

I put it to you that the word 'leadership' in this context is tantamount to influence; 'thought leader' is a well-worn phrase today and simply another way of saying influencer. If you seek Peerless Positioning, look no further than trust. We know trust can easily be broken. Achieving a level of trust is necessary, but at the same time we know that the achievement of trust is a lifelong journey and not the end goal. There are, in my opinion, core elements of building trust:

1. **Be the real you, always.** I have personally met many people I was influenced by at some point, whether it was through their sporting prowess, business acumen, or some other talent they were known for. The ones who really stick in my mind as being true influencers are the ones who were exactly the same in real life as the person I got to know, like and trust through the media and online through their content. Equally, my trust has been broken when I've come to the realisation that part of a person's public face was a show or a persona they created that was not the real them.

2. **Be honest.** I touched on the concept of polarising your tribe. Honesty in your communication will build trust by polarising your followers, who will either agree or disagree with your viewpoint. Remember, you're not looking to appeal to everyone and it's okay to upset a few people along the way. People may not always agree with what you stand for, or your point of view, but they will respect your honesty.

3. **Stick to your superpower.** In other words, stay consistent to your tribe and your message. There's no easier way to lose trust than to be unclear in your message. Building trust in a niche is your objective, not trying to appeal to everyone.

4. **Play the long game.** Right now, I'm envisioning an image I've seen many times over the years. It's an image of a miner who has buried his pick in the dirt wall in front of him and walked away, giving up on his quest for gold. Just beyond his pick, a few centimetres away, is a rich vein that would change his life forever. Don't be the miner who quits right before that huge break. Stick with it and FOCUS (Follow One Course Until Successful).

5. **Give away your best knowledge.** In most cases, people want the solution more than the know-how to get it. When I released *The LinkedIn Playbook*, many people contacted me and said something along the lines of: *I can't believe you gave away the information on how to succeed on LinkedIn. Now*

nobody needs your help to do that. You're going to lose so much money.

Of course, the opposite of this occurred. More people got to know who I was and reached out to me for those services. Thousands of people received (and are still receiving) great value from the process I shared, and many of them now refer their colleagues to my work.

WARNING: Ensure you read the upcoming chapter on Know-How *vs* No-How closely. You need to ensure you implement the concept of giving away your best knowledge correctly.

Now you have the framework for creating influence, the three pillars of influence: know, like, trust. Each of these pillars has three accelerators, and I will now explain these nine accelerators in a step-by-step process so that you, too, can become that person of influence you desire to be.

Tony Brooks

Tony helps companies automate tasks and create digital workers, meaning that teams across the world are free to do their best work, free from the mundane. He is a regular speaker, commentator, podcast guest and founder of the tech consultancy FutureAbility.

What was the biggest challenge you were having with LinkedIn before working with the Prominence Global team?

I didn't have any framework for connecting with my potential clients and didn't see value that comes from regular content sharing. Even though I knew my clients live there, I wasn't appreciative of the value of claiming the authority space amongst my connections.

How has your time spent on LinkedIn changed since joining the program?

I enjoy using the platform a lot more; I actually really enjoy putting content together and sharing it. This is great, as I'm building a tribe, and this will lead to greater things as my business grows.

Can you share one or two benefits you have experienced since joining the program?

My connections have gone through the roof; and by linking connections to B1G1, I'm also having a positive impact. The fact that we have low touch on all the admin of connecting and messaging means I have a lot more time to focus on business growth.

How has this impacted you, either personally or as results for your business?

As I write this, we're just about to relaunch the company, including a web event that we're putting together with guidance from the Prominence team. I'm super excited by this, which is a sea change from last year, where marketing was in the 'too hard basket' for me. My business will grow as a result of the work I do with Adam and the team.

Tony Brooks

www.linkedin.com/in/antothony

www.linkedin.com/company/futureability

www.futureability.io

CHAPTER 4

The Nine Accelerators of Influence

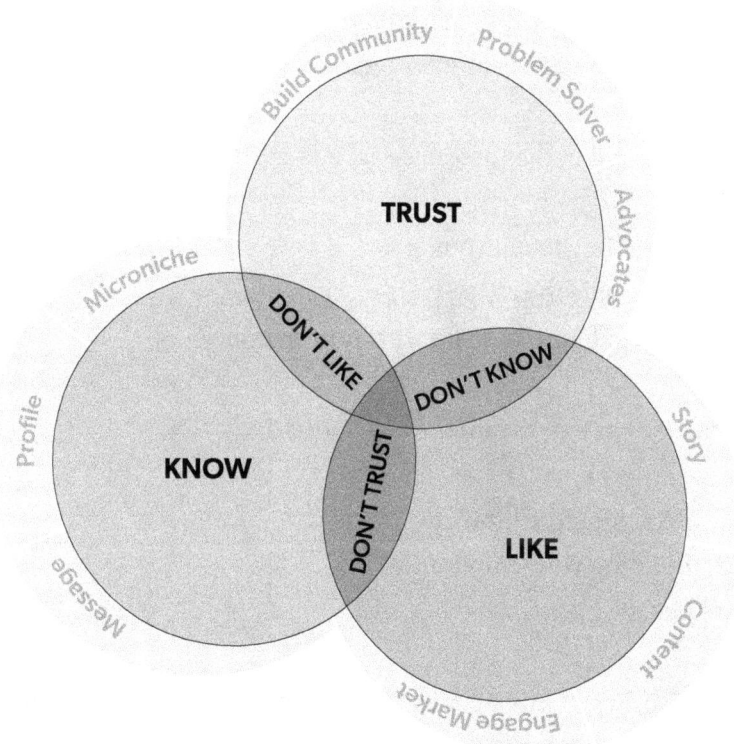

Each of the three pillars of influence has three accelerators that will enable you to achieve it. The accelerators are outlined in a deliberate order. Follow them in this order to achieve the maximum benefit and best results from this entire process. As with the three pillars— know, like, trust—the accelerators are usually attained one after the other.

For the *know* pillar, the three accelerators are:

1. Creating a microniche
2. Having an exceptional profile
3. Having a very clear message

For the *like* pillar, the three accelerators are:

1. The ability to tell your story
2. Being able to engage your market
3. The content you share with your market

For the *trust* pillar, the three accelerators are:

1. Becoming the problem solver
2. Building your community
3. Creating advocates

Of course, what this all means to each of us will vary, but the framework has been tried and tested many times over in multiple industries, countries and individual profiles. By profile, I'm referring to a simple online tool you can use to determine your own profile.

My personal favourite is the Wealth Dynamics profiling tool created by Roger Hamilton.[9] There are eight profiles within Roger's framework, and we all fall under one of them. The profiles are:

- Mechanic
- Creator
- Star
- Supporter
- Dealmaker
- Trader
- Accumulator
- Lord

No one profile is better than another. Each person's profile simply represents what they will find is their natural genius; in other words, what they do best. Many examples of well-known people are given in each category.

Before embarking on your journey to becoming an influencer, I highly recommend you use the Wealth Dynamics profiling tool to do this simple test; it is possibly the best investment in yourself you can make.

The point of this test is to give you clarity on what your natural genius is and what comes easiest to you, or, as Roger puts it: 'Why

---

9 See wealthdynamics.geniusu.com

make things hard work when you can follow your natural flow?'

I'm sure you're asking what this has to do with becoming influential, and it's a good question. Your success in this journey will be infinitely greater if you choose to become influential within the sphere of your natural talents; this is the path of least resistance.

Often this is the single greatest challenge the people I have now personally coached through this process have had to overcome. Many of these people chose to park the journey to influence until such time as they gained real clarity on the seemingly simple question I am about to ask you. It's the single most important, and therefore very first, step in your journey. It's also the reason why this is the very first of the nine accelerators, and will make or break the entire outcome for you. The question is: What is it that you want to be influential about?

Everything will flow in a logical order once you have answered this question honestly. In other words, this is your microniche. We will dive deeper into all the nine accelerators in later chapters, but for now my advice to you is to do your Wealth Dynamics test right now, before you read any further.

Once you have completed your test, and it should only take you thirty minutes to do, you will be equipped to read the next chapter, which covers the microniche in detail.

Once you have read that chapter, I would put down this book until you have some real clarity on exactly what your microniche is or could be. The remaining eight accelerators will be easier to put in place once this first step is clear in your mind.

A WORD OF WARNING: At the end of this process, when you have found out what your microniche is, you could find that you are in the wrong job, wrong business or wrong industry right now. All I can say is that it's far better to know that now, when you can start building your influence around something you truly love and will be passionate about for many years to come. It doesn't matter if you are fifteen or fifty, you have the time and ability to pivot from whatever you're doing right now to something that gives you real joy and satisfaction.

I was fifty-two years of age before I truly discovered what I wanted to do. It required a big shift in what I was doing on a daily basis and in the business I had built only a few years prior. If I could do it at fifty-two, you can do it, too. Hopefully, you will find that you're already in your flow and doing what it is you love to do, and your journey will be a breeze from here.

So, put this book aside now and either pull out your Wealth Dynamics report if you've already been through this process, or go to the URL I shared earlier and do your test. Once you have your report, really study it and understand the magic it's telling you about yourself. Then come back and read the next chapter.

'We never know which lives we influence,
or when, or why.' —**Stephen King**

Brian Sands

Brian Sands is a business problem solver, an interim executive leading organisational change, and an independent advisor to boards and executive teams designing strategy, managing risk, and creating opportunity.

His insights have been gained through frontline, hands-on and hands-in ownership and experience in high-value, high-risk, low-margin construction and property businesses. He is also the author of *Stop the Bleeding—A Mind Shift Through Business Crisis Management … Thinking and Doing Everything Differently.*

What was the biggest challenge you were having with LinkedIn before working with the Prominence Global team?

LinkedIn was a nice to have. We were not using it strategically as a business tool. It was a viewing platform of information from other people and businesses.

How has your time spent on LinkedIn changed since joining the program?

Our time is more targeted. We are posting regularly and with a longer-term content plan, connections are more refined, and have increased. Our time is spent on communicating with more valuable connections and increasing business and knowledge awareness.

Can you share one or two benefits you have experienced since joining the program?

Joining the program has built on the success of our business by creating a platform of awareness to gain more credibility, wider reach and greater recognition as an influencer and a person with expertise in business transformation.

We now have a concise plan around promoting the business, understanding how to be seen as an authority in our field, reach more individuals and potential business partners, all while giving back relevant information to followers through a variety of communication methods within LinkedIn.

We understand how to connect faster with more people and can review results of connections to make more informed decisions moving forward.

How has this impacted you, either personally or as results for your business?

Many more people have a greater understanding of our expertise in business transformation and we can see valuable partnerships forming around our specialist area of strategy and risk.

Brian Sands

www.linkedin.com/in/sandsbrian

www.briansands.com.au

CHAPTER 5

The Pyramid of Players

'The same aspirations to celebrate and uplift the spirit that drove the Egyptians to build the pyramids are still driving us. The things we're doing differently differ only in magnitude.' **—Henry Petroski**

One of the benefits of being able to release an update to a successful book is the ability to add your most up-to-date thinking to an existing, tried and proven methodology. All such tried and proven concepts evolve over time.

I'm going to share with you what has been the fundamental game changer that has evolved over the last two years in the way I see what truly happens in the journey to influence, and in particular how LinkedIn plays a hand in that journey. The 'ah-ha' moment when I first saw the patterns that emerge when you have the ability to analyse data from hundreds of profiles, and thousands of strategies that get implemented is, may I say, mind-blowing.

My own journey to this realisation dramatically changed my

beliefs of the structure of the process that has become the underlying foundation of our programs and led to a huge shift in that process. Once you grasp this, it is my belief you will have a deeper understanding of why this framework is the journey and where you currently stand. Once you know where you are, you will better know which steps are the most important for you to take next.

The journey that is

Every person I've ever spoken to at an event, in person or online, falls into one of four categories in relation to what they are doing on LinkedIn. The first step in the process is for you to honestly self-assess where you currently are positioned. As you will see there is only one place to be and the journey ahead is about reaching that pinnacle from where you are now.

The closer you are now the quicker the journey will be, but don't make the fatal mistake of talking yourself up. You are where you are, and nobody is judging. Nobody but you know, so you are best to go forward through the rest of this chapter with brutal honesty. Once you know the four levels of the pyramid, you will be able to place almost everyone you meet on LinkedIn into one of the four categories simply by looking at their profile and the content they are sharing. It's like having a crystal ball that is all-seeing and tells it as it is every time.

Of course, the only person that truly matters for you should be you, and where you rank. This will give you the insight into what you need to do to move to the top of the pyramid.

Red zone

DESPERATE TO SELL	INVISIBLE BRAND	ZERO ONLINE MARKETING SKILLS	IT'S ALL ABOUT THE PRICE

This is the base of the pyramid and if you imagine its shape, it represents the largest portion of LinkedIn members. The red zone is represented by four traits and populated by people who are displaying the number one trait: they are desperate for results and are constantly trying to sell their products or services. As far as a personal brand is concerned, they simply do not have one, and this is the second trait. We refer to it as having an 'invisible brand'.

When the world went crazy in 2020 during the full force of COVID-19, many businesses around the world were either wiped out or had their revenue decimated almost overnight. The buzzword of the day was 'pivot', referring to these businesses that were heavily impacted but still alive, and the millions of people who lost their jobs. It was a race to create an online product or service where previously a face-to-face delivery occurred, or to create an entirely new business from start-up that could be delivered remotely.

The challenge that many of these people faced was that they had no real experience or understanding of the nuances and intricacies of marketing online. This is the third trait of the red zone: no online marketing skills.

The fourth trait is that on the rare occasions people in the red zone do get someone interested in their service, whether it be a new pivot service or one that has existed for a period of time, they are constantly challenged on price. Or they are not even waiting to be challenged, their go-to strategy is to discount. Conversely the people who may be interested in the service smell blood and offer a fraction of the price requested knowing the supplier needs the sale more than they need the service.

So that's it, the red zone can be summed up by these four traits:

1. Desperate for results
2. Invisible brand
3. No marketing skills
4. Challenged on price

As I mentioned earlier, this is the time for both brutal honesty and not talking yourself up because you don't like the category you are currently in. If you are in the red zone right now, all you need to do is acknowledge that, and know you are about to undertake the journey out of this zone. Nobody is judging; nobody knows but you.

Amber zone

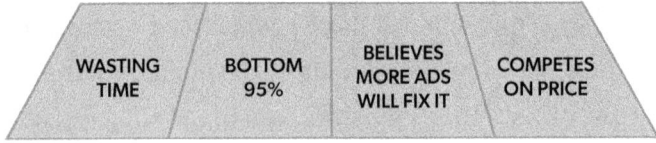

Once again there are four traits that make up the amber zone and compared to the red zone, right now it probably sounds heavenly.

I'd agree by comparison if you are here then you'll most likely being feeling relieved. It is a better place to be but it isn't the pinnacle by a long shot.

The first trait of the amber zone is you are wasting your time. By this I mean you are spending more and more time online and specifically on LinkedIn without a plan and a routine. It's easy to be distracted by the many things that there are to do, and all of the content being shared. If you often look at the time and realise an hour just disappeared, and it's an hour you are never getting back because you cannot think of anything tangible you achieved during it, welcome to the amber zone.

Thankfully something intangible that you've started creating is a personal brand, but it's not yet rock solid and something you are quite proud of. We define this as having a brand in the bottom 95 percent and this is the second trait. I know that sounds harsh, but the online world is a hyper-competitive and ruthless place. Think of industries such as elite sports, music or dance. Millions of people want to be amongst the A players, yet the incontestable truth is that only the top 5 percent make a living from it, and a very small fraction of that top 5 percent make 95 percent of the money.

The third trait of the amber zone is a belief that you can buy your way out. Interestingly, to some degree, this is true. It is possible to spend huge amounts of money in online advertising and many people will tell you this is the fastest way to online success. I'm not suggesting this is not a valid strategy; it can be. But what if you don't have the ad budget to play the 'those who spend most win' game?

This is what we refer to as 'increasing ad spend'. If you ask anybody who is relying heavily on Facebook advertising as a strategy, they will tell you that generally speaking, getting the same results today in relation to CPC (cost per click) as they did a year or two ago costs more than it did back then.

Equally ask anyone who invests in Google Ads and they will tell you some horror stories, depending on how competitive their industry is online. It's no accident that Google is now a multi-billion-dollar company on the back of the revenue they generate through Google Ads. Quite simply, it's an auction for online traffic, those who spend the most win.

People in the amber zone are getting results, despite their brand not being strong. They need to keep spending more and more to get those results. As a natural progression of this, they are competing on price and this is the fourth trait.

Unlike those in the red zone, they have a more consistent flow of enquiries through their marketing, yet they are still seen as a commodity whereby there are plenty of other options if the enquirer thinks they can get a better deal.

The amber zone can be summed up by these four traits:

1. Wasting time
2. Brand in the bottom 95 percent
3. Increasing ad spend
4. Competing on price

Green zone

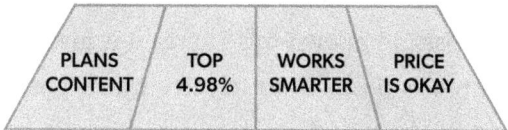

While technically speaking not the pinnacle of our pyramid, the green zone is where many people aspire to be. When I speak to those who are in this zone a common line of thinking is what we call 'blissfully self-satisfied'. That is until someone bursts your bubble and whispers in your ear that there is another level to the game, but only a very small, elite group get an invite.

The green zone is a successful place to be and let's face it, you are just below the summit and doing much better than the high majority of people in the red and amber zones. You are seeing a positive ROI (return on investment) on your LinkedIn efforts.

The key differentiator between the green zone and those below is having a content strategy; this is trait number one. The good news is in the coming chapters I'm going to share with you exactly what that looks like and how you too can create your own strategic content that positions you well above the pack.

People in this zone have also refined their personal brands to be in the top 4.98 percent. You can spot these profiles quite easily: they look professional, they act professionally, and they have amazing content that is highly engaged. They are often envied by many and rightly so. This is the second trait of the green zone.

The third trait is while those in this zone are doing well, they also continue to work harder and harder to maintain their position here. It becomes almost like an addiction, something attained and to be protected at all costs; in many ways I agree it is just that.

The fourth trait is they do not receive much push back on the pricing of their products and services, which really is a great place to be. This doesn't mean they win every enquiry; nobody truly does that. Yet they win more often than they lose, and their conversations are rarely about price, they are about value.

The green zone can be summed as by these four traits:

1. Strategic content creation
2. Brand in the top 4.98 percent
3. Working harder
4. Accepted pricing

Light-green zone

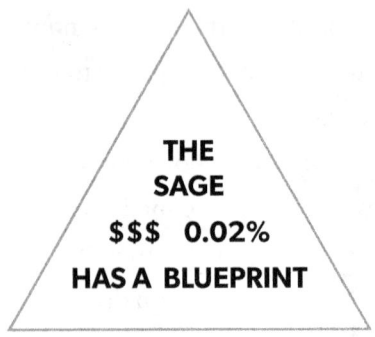

THE
SAGE
$$$ 0.02%
HAS A BLUEPRINT

This is the pinnacle because very few people reach it, and reaching this coveted place comes with some very special privileges. Once again there are four traits that denote membership to this club. The first is what we refer to as 'sage-like positioning': they are very well known in their industry. These are the people who are constantly contacted for interviews and to be a speaker at conferences, a guest on podcasts and invited to VIP events. Interestingly enough, they are also the ones LinkedIn reaches out to and invites to share their opinions on new products or to join closed groups that get access to information nobody else has access to.

I'm sure you were wondering why the green zone represented the top 4.98 percent of brands. In simple terms, it is because that final 0.02 percent is held by the light-green zone, and this is the second trait. These are world-class personal brands that other companies and people want to be associated with.

Unlike the third trait in the green zone (working harder), in the light-green zone they have what we refer to as a 'systemised marketing blueprint'. It's a marketing machine that is built on the personal brand and requires no ad spend; it is implemented by a team and it works, it really works.

Price is never a conversation, only value, yet it is so much more than that. The people in the light-green zone are also those who have their products and services priced in the top one percent in their industry. They can regularly update their prices and it's never questioned, as people desperately want to work with these industry leaders and while of course they want to see a return on their investment with them, they rarely consider another service because their price is lower.

Getting to this position does require that your products and services really are world class; these people are not faking it until they make it. You will see glowing recommendations about them on their LinkedIn profiles and websites from happy customers and they get a high volume of referred clients coming from existing clients.

The light-green zone can be summed as by these four traits:

1. Sage-like positioning
2. Brands in the top 0.02 percent
3. Systemised marketing blueprint
4. Top one percent industry pricing

As I mentioned at the start of this chapter, coming to the realisation of these four zones changed everything we do and how we do it. The rest of the coming chapters are your step-by-step guide to the light-green zone.

Read it!

Implement it!

The magic will happen!

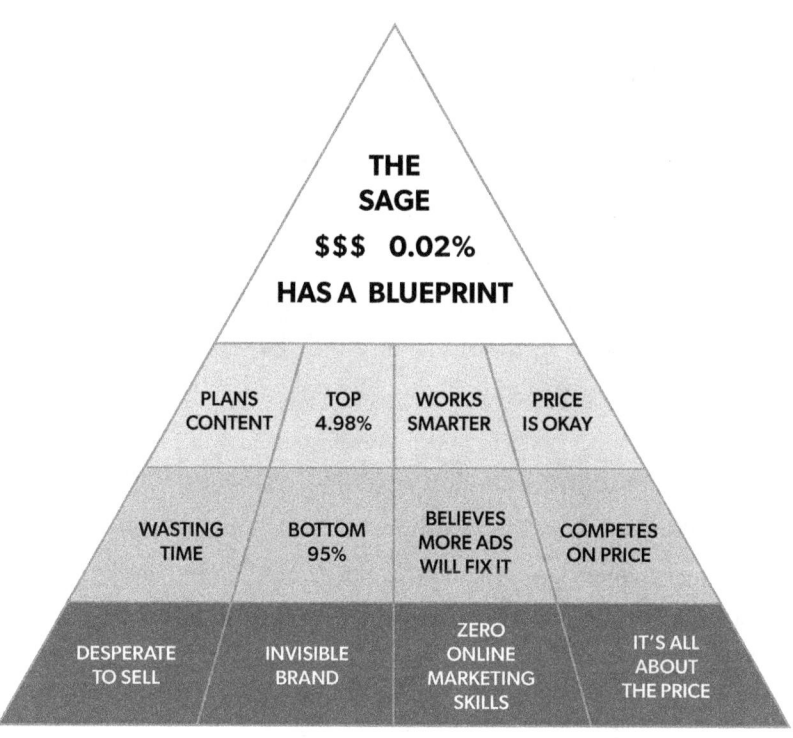

Archana Shetty

Archana is an executive leadership coach and mentor. Her expertise is in emotional intelligence and peak performance. She is the CEO of WELead Coaching & Consulting, a consultancy company that specialises in leadership, team building and culture transformation.

She helps medium- to large-sized tech companies and start-ups maximise their potential and achieve exceptional business results by building resilient, collaborative teams and helping leaders operate at their highest level of contribution so that they can build companies where people love to work.

What was the biggest challenge you were having with LinkedIn before working with the Prominence Global team?
My biggest challenge was I felt I was not visible and did not know how to stand out in a crowded market of many coaches and consultants. It was frustrating.

How has your time spent on LinkedIn changed since joining the program?
Most of my time now on LinkedIn is responding to messages and sharing content. My connections are more targeted and niche now.

Can you share one or two benefits you have experienced since joining the program?

With feedback from the team, I have updated my LinkedIn profile. I have an all-star profile and my connection acceptance percentage is above average. I understand the strategy to stand out in a crowded market. It has helped build relationships with prospects and get clients.

How has this impacted you, either personally or as results for your business?

Targeted niche and consistency in content sharing has built up my credibility. I am seen as a trusted advisor in my space. Hopefully, a thought leader soon. Also, the events I create get a higher number of sign-ups.

Archana Shetty

www.linkedin.com/in/archananshetty

www.linkedin.com/company/welead-coaching-and-consulting

welead-coaching.com

CHAPTER 6

Creating Your Microniche

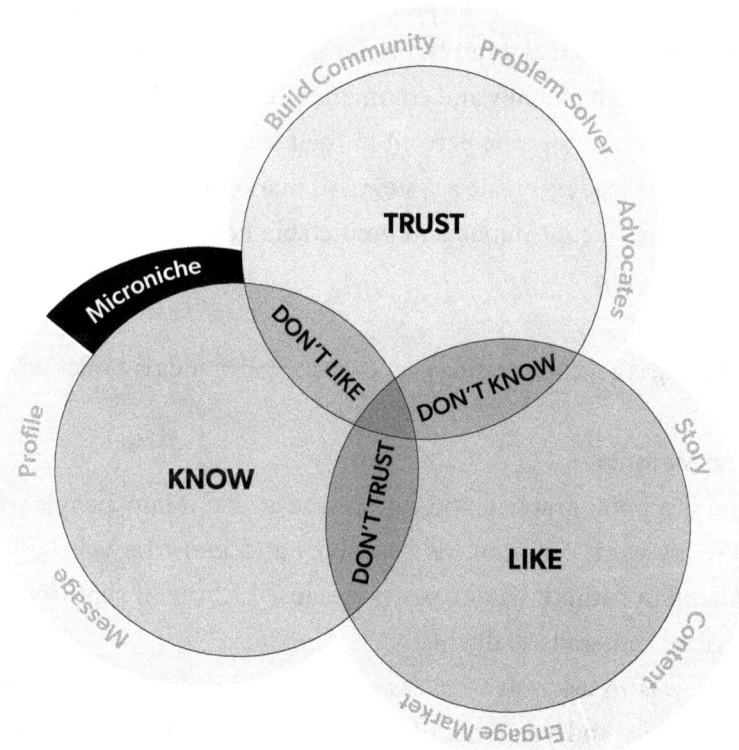

Let's start by getting clear on exactly what a microniche is. To do that I'm going to use myself and my company and two good friends of mine as examples: Jason Malouin and Shane Saunders.

Now that you have read the previous chapter, you might come to the realisation that we are not just a marketing agency; this would be much too broad a niche. We don't even consider ourselves a LinkedIn agency, believe it or not. We are hopefully getting the message out to the world that what we do is the following:

We help business leaders attain sage-like positioning through peerless personal brands on LinkedIn that sit in the top 0.02 percent globally and command pricing for their services that is in the top one percent in their industry. We also help business leaders create a systemised marketing blueprint that generates a continuous and predictable flow of leads month after month.

Marketing is a niche; creating peerless personal brands is a microniche.

Jason Malouin

Jason is a photographer, and a great one at that. Many people who know his work can spot his headshots and know he was behind the camera without having to ask because his way of capturing an image on camera is so distinct.

If I was to ask you what Jason's niche is, you would likely say photography and you would be correct. But in terms of influence, this niche is too broad, and we need to drill down into that niche to narrow the focus. For Jason to dominate the entire photography niche, he would be competing against every form of photography that exists, including aerial, fashion, pinhole, landscape, cityscape, nature, wildlife, wedding, black and white, travel, underwater, sunrise/sunset, storm, bird and portrait, just to name a few. Becoming influential in such a broad sense is extremely difficult.

Jason's superpower, what he is known and highly respected for, is headshot photography. This is his microniche, upon which he has built his influence.[10]

Shane Saunders

Shane Saunders is a coach, and not just any coach; specifically, he is a breathing coach. He doesn't coach people in sports, mindset, business, music, cheerleading, life, wellness, career, relationships, sales or motivation. Although these all come under the niche of coaching, Shane is a breathing coach. That's right, he trains entrepreneurs to breathe properly so they can achieve what Shane calls 'peak state'. Shane's niche is coaching, and his microniche is breath coaching for entrepreneurs.

Shane is my breathing coach and I can tell you from experience that his has been one of the most impactful training programs I have ever undertaken.[11]

You can see from these examples that a microniche is a niche within a niche. Photography is a broad niche and headshot photographer

---

10 You can meet Jason on LinkedIn at www.linkedin.com/in/jasonmalouin
11 You can meet Shane on LinkedIn at www.linkedin.com/in/shane-saunders

is a laser-focused microniche. Coach is a broad niche and breathing coach for entrepreneurs is a laser-focused microniche.

Like Shane, I am also a coach, and given my previous books my niche is probably social media. Of course, that's much too broad. You could refine that to being an authority on LinkedIn, but again that's too broad. After all, there are many well-respected and talented people in the world who also know how to leverage LinkedIn like I do.

For me, a niche could be coaching influence, but that category should also be narrowed down. I would say that my microniche is more specific than that: I coach people to be influential using LinkedIn.

What is your microniche?

By now I have asked this question of the people I coach hundreds and hundreds of times. Often it's not easy to see the micropotential within a category. One such industry is real estate. The question asked of real-estate agents is usually: How much more niche can I be than to say I'm a real-estate agent focused on residential properties?

Residential real estate is a broad niche. An example of a microniche within that broad niche could be specialising in finding under-priced residential investment properties in Brisbane between $700,000 and $1 million for investors with self-managed super funds. This microniche will move the real-estate agent out of the crowded space of the broader real-estate industry.

As we move through the other eight accelerators, you will see that it becomes easier to create content, have a clear marketing message, and build a specific tribe or advocates than if the niche was simply residential real-estate agent.

As an FYI, in 2020 there were over 300,000 real-estate agents on LinkedIn. As of late 2022, that number has increased to 1,590,000. But how many of those agents specialise in finding under-priced residential investment properties in Brisbane between $700,000 and $1 million for investors with self-managed super funds?

Now you have four clear examples of microniches: Jason, the headshot legend; Shane, the breathing coach; Adam, the influence-on-LinkedIn dude; and a real-estate agent who is your go-to person for investment properties in Brisbane.

I can almost hear you thinking up your next question, and yes, we have covered that question hundreds of times, too. It's something along the lines of: *But if I only focus on headshot photography, or investment properties between $700,000 and $1 million, won't I be missing out on lots of opportunities in other forms of photography or real estate, and what happens if I find a great investment property for someone that is only $600,000?*

There is a well-known saying that covers this: 'If you try to appeal to everybody, you appeal to nobody.'

Jason does plenty of photo shoots of people that are more than just headshots; Shane makes a ton of money from group-based corporate-training days. I do a lot more than just coach influence on LinkedIn (in fact, our main revenue comes from managing the LinkedIn profiles of highly influential people). And even our real-estate agent sells plenty of properties for less than $700,000 or more than $1 million, and to homeowners as often as investors.

The point of the microniche is to make you stand out in a crowded space, and to make it much easier to be influential within that chosen space. Finding your microniche will rarely hinder you; in fact, I would say that in almost all cases it will grow your revenue.

The best type of microniche will combine your greatest passion (something that is in your natural flow as long as it's something you can generate an income from), with the opportunity to create a business, product or service around that passion. It's the intersection of passion, expertise and opportunity.

The Wealth Dynamics profile test

In the last chapter I suggested you take the Wealth Dynamics profile test if you have never done so before. The point of the exercise is to fully understand what flow means for you. Like most of us, you probably have more than one passion, and the test will help you hone in on a particular passion that you already have a great talent for. It will also help you build your knowledge around that natural flow and love for your chosen area of expertise.

Before jumping right in and being 100 percent convinced that this passion is your chosen path or your calling, ask yourself another question: Can I build a business, product or service that will monetise my passion? It will need to be within your ability to generate income from this passion. Otherwise you risk splitting your time between your non-paying passion, and the day job that generates your income. Or worse, slowly going broke while loving what you do every day.

I've met many successful entrepreneurs who make a good living but have no sense of fulfilment in their careers or joy in their lives, because they have always been in pursuit of the money that comes from what they do. I have also met many people who live for their passion, but struggle to pay the bills because they haven't developed a powerful way to productise their gift. Believe me, you don't want to be in this space.

In the last chapter I also suggested that you read to the end of this chapter and then put the book aside until you have a rock-solid grasp of the microniche you want to move forward with. You also need to have an idea of the product, service or business you want to develop. It could be exactly what you're doing right now, and if that's the case then read on and get the next steps done as quickly as you can.

If you're not living your passion right now and want to use this book to take the first steps in this journey, my best advice is not to get too concerned about having everything in place in the next ninety days. Take your time to really consider this next step and get it right.

Most likely you'll find that you're not the first person to come up with your idea. That doesn't mean you should throw it out and look for something you've never done before.

If we take the example of our real-estate agent, would it matter if someone else were doing something similar in Sydney, New York or London? The price point in those locations would likely be much higher than $700,000, but no, it wouldn't matter at all.

What matters is that you choose something you are truly passionate about, enough to spend many of your waking hours doing, that you can generate an income from, and that it gives you the opportunity to own this space in your city or your industry.

Once you have your passion, and are considering how you might productise it, do some global research. You will probably find that someone has done it before you. While I'm not suggesting that you replicate their product or service, it should give you some comfort to know that you can create a marketable and viable product.

If you can't find even one example of someone doing something the same, or similar, to what you're considering, I suggest you think hard about it. The world is full of people with a great idea before its time. Don't be the property developer who builds a new subdivision five years before the market is ready for it.

Hopefully, you already have a fair idea of what you plan to do from here or, even better, that you're lucky enough to already be doing it. From this point on, I'm going to make the assumption that you have this step sorted. Each of the following chapters should be read on the basis that you have clarity about what it is you will be building your influence for.

'If everybody is doing it one way, there a good
chance you can find your niche by going exactly
in the opposite direction.' **—Sam Walton**

Caroline Jean-Baptiste

Caroline Jean-Baptiste isn't your average mortgage broker. She is an author, business owner, and mentor. Her business, Mortgage Choice in Fortitude Valley, Queensland, Australia, has helped thousands of people get a loan, buy their home, and create choice, flexibility and control over their future.

Her book *Buy That House—How Kickass Women Make It Happen* is an inspirational guide that teaches women how to connect with their cashflow, save a deposit and buy that house. Caroline is regularly acknowledged for business excellence within the mortgage-broking industry and was awarded the Abundance Global Profitability Award in 2018.

What was the biggest challenge you were having with LinkedIn before working with the Prominence Global team?
I was looking to build my profile and connect with more customers and I just wasn't getting the traction through my regular channels.

How has your time spent on LinkedIn changed since joining the program?
I now have a more structured and purposeful approach with consistency in my message and increased connections.

Can you share one or two benefits you have experienced since joining the program?

Being in front of my customers and prospects regularly and sharing a consistent message means that I can connect with the right customers and build a targeted network.

The program has kept me accountable, made me more consistent on social media and helped me develop my skills on camera.

How has this impacted you, either personally or as results for your business?

With a more structured approach to my LinkedIn strategy, it means I save time and don't just scroll through wondering what I should do. The professional approach has brought more leads and has been a great way to build a strong network.

Caroline Jean-Baptiste

www.linkedin.com/in/carolinejeanbaptiste1

www.mortgagechoice.com.au/caroline.jean-baptiste

CHAPTER 7

Your Influencer Profile

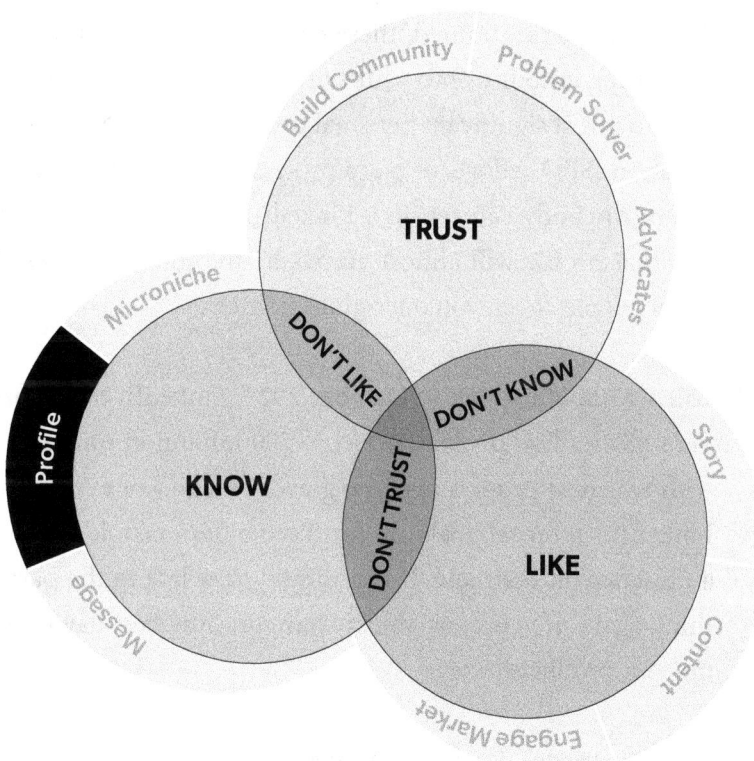

I believe that one of the most important tools everyone, from the age of eighteen upwards, can invest in is their LinkedIn profile, regardless of whether they choose to use that presence to become an influencer in the sense of what I'm sharing in this book or not. There are three reasons to consider a LinkedIn profile.

5. **It's free.** Unlike creating your own personal website, which, even if you possess the skills to do it yourself, entails hosting expenses, and ongoing expenses for ownership of your domain name/s. Granted, these costs can be quite minimal, but getting visibility onto your site will not be. You will either need to invest significant personal time in search engine optimisation (SEO) efforts or pay a professional for their time to do so. Anybody can set up a LinkedIn profile at no charge, and that profile will almost always be the top search result when people check you out online.

6. **You are not alone.** As of October 2022, LinkedIn had more than 850 million profiles, up from 700 million in mid-2020, with two new profiles appearing every second of every day. LinkedIn's internal goals are for three billion people to have a presence on their site. If you think you're late to the party, think again. If you don't already have one, the best day to set up your profile is today.

7. **It's easy to do.** Realistically, you can have an acceptable presence within a few hours. Every one of those current and

future three billion profiles has access to exactly the same tools and format that you do, whether they are the world's best-known industry heavyweights or eighteen-year-old students completing their final year of school.

Creating an exceptional profile

Everyone can have All Star status as part of their LinkedIn profile, but that flash-sounding category simply means they have completed all the sections of their profile. It doesn't necessarily mean that they've completed them well. It is, however, important to make sure that you do have an All Star rated profile to ensure that LinkedIn shows you the best searches.

Creating an exceptional profile will take a little more effort, but it's essential if you wish to become an influencer so let's dive right into that process now.

If your profile status is *Beginner, Intermediate, Advanced* or *Expert*, it's an indication that you've missed one or more of the following important steps (I will cover these in depth shortly). To update the first seven areas, not including images, you need to go to your home page and click on the pencil icon in the upper-right area just below the background image. This will give you access to key categories, all of which you will need to complete.

- Background image
- Profile image
- Professional headline

- Pronouns
- Current position/experience
- Industry
- Education
- Location
- Contact info
- Creator Mode
- Services you provide
- Featured
- Skills and endorsements
- Recommendations

Now let's dive a little deeper into some of these critical areas of your profile, and more.

Background image

This is the very top section of your profile and by default it's set to the standard light blue image you will see on many profiles. No influencers will leave this section on the default setting. It's imperative that you create a personalised background image to replace the default setting. If you have some reasonable skills in graphic design, you can certainly give this a go yourself. If not, Canva[12] is a great online tool you might choose to use to create your background image.

The dimensions you need to use can be found by going to your home page and clicking on the pencil icon in the upper-right area of the background image. This will give you the most

---

12 canva.com

up-to-date dimensions required since LinkedIn tends to change these occasionally.

You should also take note of where your profile image is currently displayed because this will appear over any text or images you have on your background image. So make sure you format your background image with this in mind.

We have developed a template tool that makes the formatting very simple. You are very welcome to a free download available from our Facebook group.[13]

Once again, I'm reading your mind and quite likely you are thinking, *Why does he have his community on Facebook if everything he's suggesting we build our influence within is LinkedIn?* At the very top of the Facebook group feed, you will find a video from me that explains this for you. Make sure you watch that video to answer this important question.

I highly recommend that you outsource the creation of your background image to a professional graphic designer. If you don't have a relationship with someone who can do this, you can easily connect with someone who specialises in graphic design for LinkedIn on sites like Fiverr[14] or Freelancer.[15]

I also suggest you spend some time scrolling through different profiles on LinkedIn until you find one or two that you personally resonate with and then brief your designer according to the style of

---

13 To access it, simply join our online community at www.facebook.com/groups/
   LinkedIn2Success

14 www.fiverr.com

15 www.freelancer.com

image you would like. A good option would be to use something similar to your company or personal website home page, if appropriate, to keep alignment with your branding.

Profile image

Equally important as the background image is your profile image. The best type of image is a headshot of yourself. Under no circumstances should this be a logo of your business, which should be part of your background image.

This is something you may choose to do yourself, but it's also worth spending a few hundred dollars for a professional photographer. If you do decide to use a photo you already have, or that a friend or family member has taken for you, ensure that it's shot in a well-lit area with a clear background. It's highly unlikely that the selfie you took on the weekend is going to be good-enough quality, and always keep in mind that this is the first impression of you that people will have.

I also suggest you update this photo every couple of years at the very least. There's nothing that destroys the trust factor (see later chapter on this) quicker than having a face-to-face or online meeting with someone you've connected with, only for them to discover that you're ten or more years older than your profile suggests, or significantly heavier or lighter in weight, or you now sport a new beard or are clean shaven, or have a completely new hair colour or style.

Believe me, I'm speaking from experience in all of these examples. It's imperative that you update your profile image if any of these examples are relevant for you now or in the future.

Professional headline

This is the area directly under your profile image and is one of the areas most likely to be read on your profile. This is your opportunity to give people a good first impression of what you're all about and why they might want to connect with you. I recommend completing this section in one of two ways. You could write a short sentence that outlines who you best serve and how you serve them, or use specific keywords that showcase your areas of influence and expertise. Or you could use a mixture of both, which you will often find is how mine is showing. You only need to have a very small character count to use here—220, to be exact—so you need to be succinct and clear in your message.

Pronouns

You can now choose to add personal pronouns beside your name to reflect how you wish to be addressed, i.e., He/Him, She/Her, or They/Them. Additionally, you can also choose the Custom option, which allows you to add your chosen terms.

For some people wishing to express, confirm, or reinforce their gender identity, this is a positive option.

Creator Mode

This is a big plus in my view, as you can now extend how you wish to be seen and engaged with. From your home page, scroll down to the Resources section. There, you will see Creator Mode with an option have this set as ON or OFF. When set to ON, you then enter an area where you can add up to five hashtags to your profile based on what you mostly write about. This makes it easier for people to find you based on your key topics and areas of expertise. The hashtags you select will appear in the top part of your profile, so anyone visiting can see these clearly.

In addition, you can also enable access to the following set of tools:

- Newsletters: With newsletters, you can regularly publish articles about a specific topic and build a subscriber base. You must have 150 or more followers or connections, a history of posting relevant and original expertise-based posts and articles, and abide by LinkedIn's community standards to enable newsletters. (See more on newsletters on page 96.)

- Audio Events: These can be up to three hours long, and anyone can attend them. Simply enable Audio Events if you are eligible—having 150 or more followers or connections, following LinkedIn's community standards, and a history of posting relevant and original content—and set the time and date for your event. To create the event, specify this as an AUDIO option in your event set-up area. You can then share this as a post to promote it. You can also invite your connections to attend. Your attendees can engage with your event by posing questions, and listen in even with the page minimised.

- LinkedIn Live: This takes the Audio Event option to another level by allowing you to plan, promote and then live-stream a video event for invited attendees. These events are also publicly searchable, and you can add a registration to your event so you know who and how many are attending. An additional benefit of this is your ability to add registrants to your newsletter database.

With Creator Mode you can extend the option of having people simply follow you, which is not the same as being connected to you. A connection requires you to both be engaged in knowing each other, where an invitation to connect is given and accepted. Followers are people who might also be connections, but may be simply people who like what you share and want to follow only your content and updates without being mutually connected.

Open to Work

You can add a badge to your profile photo indicating you are available for work-related opportunities, and set up an additional port in your profile connecting this. Simply go to the Open to Work tab in the upper section of your profile and select Finding a New Job from the drop-down options. From there you can add preferences such as ideal job titles, locations, whether you'd prefer remote or on-site work, and whether you're looking for full-time, part time, contract, or even temporary work options. You can also choose whether all LinkedIn members can see you're open for work, or whether this is private to only those members using LinkedIn Recruiter.

Services you provide

This sits beside the Open to Work tab in the upper section of your profile and enables you to list the expertise and services you have to offer. Inside this section you can list up to ten services, invite past clients to review you based on those services listed, and feature media such as videos and interviews that showcase your abilities.

Contact info

You need to click the pencil icon under your background image near the top right of your profile to access this area. Once you're there, the first item to update is your profile URL. Again, by default LinkedIn will give you a terrible profile URL with a whole string of irrelevant numbers on the end.

Click the link to your URL, which will take you to another page with your public profile settings. In the top right you'll see the section to edit and personalise your URL. Click the pencil icon here; you can change your profile URL to anything you choose as long as it's not being used by somebody else. I would make this as simple and short as you can (mine is now www.linkedin.com/in/ adamhoulahan).

While you're in this section, the next thing to do is click the option to make your profile visible to the public. You should also make public every aspect of the profile you can see here. Even if you only intend to operate in one country, activate the machine-translated profile option.

Once you're finished here, return to the contact information section and complete as many of the options to have your details open to the public as you are comfortable with.

Summary

Sometimes called your About section or your LinkedIn bio, this is one of the most important areas to utilise well. The character count here is just 2,600 and you'll likely need every one of them. I suggest you take a look at mine as an example, but here's the framework we use to create this section:

- Your name
- Your claim to fame
- Your insight
- The result you will deliver
- Your experience
- The problems your clients face
- How you solve those problems
- Your personal *why*
- Your impact
- A call to action

This is a lot to cover, so you'll need to be succinct and spare the buzzwords.

I'm still surprised by how many people leave this section blank, or do a very poor job of giving the people who visit their profile the opportunity they need to get to know them. Make this your best work or outsource it to a professional copywriter.

Featured

You also have the opportunity to add links to websites or videos below your summary. Take the opportunity to add at least one or two pieces of high-quality external media that highlight your expertise and what you do. Very few areas within your profile allow you to add links that take people off LinkedIn, but this is the most visible section where you can do this.

This is also a great section to utilise when you have something specific to promote, such as an upcoming webinar or live event. Alternatively, you could post lead magnets to bring people to your database, such as a free course, a scorecard or a free download of some description.

Current position/Experience

This is the area most people use to list every job they've ever had, back to when they had a paper run as a student. You will use this very differently. This is where your profile will really stand out from the hundreds of millions of profiles that will never generate influence or revenue for their owner.

Once again, to gain an insight into what I outline here, take a look at my profile. You'll see very little previous job history; although I mention in my summary that I've run six businesses throughout my career, there's no mention of most of them except my current business, Prominence Global. What you will see in support of this business is what creates influence: my books and my web event that has grown into one of the world's largest free LinkedIn training events. Over 15,000 people now access these five live web events each year. So, it makes sense to highlight this front and centre on my profile.

I highly recommend that you do something similar. Have one entry about your business, and one about your product or service. If you've written a book, add another entry that outlines information about the book, provided it has some alignment with your business, product or service.

You only have 2,000 characters, but you now have 2,000 characters for each of the sections you add as part of your experience. You can use these to outline your past experiences like you would on a resume, like the vast majority of LinkedIn members do, or you can use them to go more deeply into what you do now and your real expertise.

I have already mentioned, but it's worth stating again, that in this area, where everyone on LinkedIn has the opportunity to do as they please, more than 99 percent do what everyone else is doing. Consequently, they miss the potential this simple process gives them to become influential in their industry by using LinkedIn as their platform.

Education

You need to complete this section or your profile will not be All Star. It doesn't have to contain your formal education but be sure to add something. It might be a training course you completed or a significant online course. If you never completed high school, don't worry. You are not alone. You might be surprised to know I was expelled in my last year of high school and never looked back.

I'd go as far as to say it was the most value I received from my school years.

Later in life, I did complete a business degree but as you can see from my profile, I placed the greatest value in the Key Person of Influence program I completed through the Dent organisation. It is important you add something in this section so even if you add something like 'graduated from the school of hard knocks', that's fine.

You can also add links to media or websites here if you choose.

Skills and endorsements

This area is one of the most misunderstood LinkedIn profile options. You absolutely need to activate this area of your profile, and you need to choose your skills wisely. Don't think of them as skills you may possess, such as hobbies or job skills. Instead, think of them as keywords you would want people to use in their searches. The top three are your most important since they are visible on your profile to people who come across you or choose to search for you. The rest are there to be viewed, but visitors will have to click the Show More tab to access them.

Often, I speak to people who share that they were hell-bent on reaching what they thought was the maximum ninety-nine-plus endorsements for each these skills and then stopped worrying about them. Something you should really know about the true value of skills and endorsements is that LinkedIn does use this area in deciding what searches to show you in, so it's important you have good skills listed. If you think about that, it makes sense. We can talk all we like about ourselves and what we believe we provide real value in, but nothing beats the opinion from others. (I'll cover this in depth in an upcoming chapter about tribes.)

Accomplishments

In this section you have many options, and I don't suggest that you complete all of them simply for the sake of having them on your profile. Choose the ones that will help position you as both credible and influential—with one exception: languages. Make sure this one is active. The optional inclusions are:

- Licenses and certification
- Courses
- Volunteer experience
- Publications
- Patents
- Projects
- Honours and awards
- Test scores
- Languages
- Organisations
- Causes

If you've written a book or books, or even had an industry paper published, list them here. The same goes for any awards, which are well worth showcasing.

Interests

These are broken into three categories:

- LinkedIn Influencers
- Companies
- Groups

Any of these you choose to follow on LinkedIn will appear here, so make sure they're in alignment with your beliefs or, more importantly, the beliefs you want to have on show to the public.

Recommendations

There is another important section of your profile, and that is recommendations. This is covered in depth in a later chapter, but for now it's essential to know that you should have an ongoing strategy to increase your recommendations on your profile. There's no magic number of recommendations to have, but there is one number you don't want and that is zero.

You can only receive recommendations from people you are linked to on LinkedIn as first-degree connections. I don't recommend that you engage in the practice of swapping recommendations (i.e., I'll do one for you if you do one for me). There is no credibility in doing this, and keep in mind that anyone viewing your recommendations can link to all the profiles of the people who have given them, as well as those you have given to others.

On occasion, people will voluntarily do you the honour of giving you a recommendation. If you've gone out of your way to create an exceptional outcome for a client, by all means ask them if they would be open to supplying a recommendation on your profile. If you click on their profile link, you will find an option in the More section to request a recommendation. Make it easy for them by sending them a request for one here. It will also give you the option to select how you have worked together.

Follow these steps and you will have the exceptional profile that all influencers have, or at least should have.

Creating an exceptional Company Page

If you have a personal LinkedIn personal profile that is well populated and you have—or are at least well on your way to having—an All Star ranking, then you may like to consider supporting your profile with a Company Page. This is about further profiling yourself and promoting your influence-ability.

You may have noticed when you look at someone's profile, that in their Experience section, some listings feature logos and live links to company LinkedIn profiles. Having a page and profile for your company with a live link in your main personal profile area helps lead more people to your main area of business. Just as in the real world, your business venue is where the main engine room is located.

A Company Page allows you to build and grow your brand's image, connect with your current and future clients, and share company-specific news and updates. You can use a Company Page to highlight how many employees you have and their specialisations, any awards your company has won, featured documents and events, and manage your events—and that's just the start.

Some of the key tabs on a Company Page menu are:

- Home: This gives an overview of your company's whole profile. It shows a short version of your company's About section, your newsletter and a link to subscribe, upcoming events, any lead generation options you are using, community hashtags, and your latest articles, posts, or videos.
- About: This opens up your company's full About section. It also gives details about the company, including contact details, size and number of employees, locations, your industry and any specialities your company has.
- Products: Companies in certain eligible industries can use this section to highlight and showcase their products.
- Posts: This is where all company posts and articles can be found.
- Jobs: If you are seeking new employees or specific job opportunities exist within your organisation, you can post job listings here for free.
- People: Those who work for you are featured here, with links to their respective LinkedIn profiles. This section also gives demographic information about employees, such as where they are located, where and what they studied, and their professional skills.
- Events: If you have upcoming events scheduled on LinkedIn,

they will be featured here. Visitors can choose to view an event, which will give them more detail about the event, including how to register to attend. Past events remain listed on this page for visitors to view.

- Videos: Any videos you have shared about your company are featured here.

Setting up your Company Page

To create a LinkedIn Company Page and profile, simply click on the Work tab, located to the right of the Me tab, in the very top navigation bar of your LinkedIn page. The last item on the drop-down menu is Create a Company Page.

You'll then be offered three options for pages you can create: Company, Showcase, or an Educational Institution. A Showcase Page is a sub-page that you can connect to an existing LinkedIn Company Page to highlight a specific initiative or product line within your company's portfolio, while an Educational Institution Page is the best option for schools or universities. You will want to select the Company option.

Next, you'll be asked to fill in some important details about your company, such as your company name, website, what industry your company is in, and how many employees your company has. You'll be able to choose a LinkedIn URL for your Company Page here; it's best if your URL is your company name for brand consistency. You also have the option of uploading a company logo and a short 120–character tagline explaining briefly what your company does. While these are optional, I recommend including both of these to set your Company Page apart from others and reinforce your branding, your company's why, and what problem you solve for clients. Click the Create Page button.

Next, you will be taken to your new Company Page dashboard, where you will be prompted to add in more details about your company. LinkedIn provides a helpful checklist at the top of this page of steps you should complete for a successful Company Page, but there are a few you should focus on first.

- Description. This is similar to the Summary section of your personal profile. Describe your company in more detail, including the problems your clients face, how your company solves these problems, and the results your company delivers. Include relevant keywords to help people search for and discover your page. Don't forget to include a call to action at the end. You have 2,000 characters for this section.
- Location. You can add multiple locations here, but you should have at least one location listed. Even if your company is entirely online, including a location gives page visitors a clearer vision of your company.
- Cover image. Just like your background image on your personal profile, the Company Page cover image is crucial for engaging visitors and potential clients. It's imperative that you create a personalised cover image for your company to replace the default setting. You can create this yourself, or use an online tool like Canva. You can use your company's branding for this, or an image promoting a company campaign or upcoming event.

Once you have your basic Company Page set up, you can start exploring the unique page features that will elevate your message, your company, and your impact as an influencer. Read on to learn more about key features and how to use them.

Lead generation form

You can use a lead generation form to collect and track high quality leads easily. On your Company Page dashboard, click the Edit Page button just to the bottom right of the cover image area. This will open a pop-up screen where you will see a list of things you can edit. Under Leads, click on Lead Gen Form and you will be taken to a page where you can set this option as ON or OFF. Once you change this to ON, you will be able to create and customise your lead generation form.

Here, you can choose one of four calls to action (CTA): contact sales, request free demo, start free trial, or get started. Which CTA will generate the most leads for you will depend on your industry and what your company offers.

You must add a link to your company's privacy policy before you can continue.

Next, personalise your form with a short, catchy headline (maximum 50 characters) and a brief description (maximum 200 characters) of what you're offering people who submit this form— what are you giving them in exchange for their details?

With so few characters means you need to keep your offer brief and tight, but think through exactly what you want to achieve and direct your visitor clearly with this option.

Hashtags

You can add up to three primary hashtags to your Company Page to build your community, encourage visitors to engage with your posts, and further assist in searchability around your topic and industry. Choose hashtags that are relevant and well-suited to your business and specialist areas. If you're unsure of which hashtags to use, there are a number of hashtag analytics sites and tools you might use.

Newsletters

While you can create a newsletter from your personal page (see chapter 12), you can also create a newsletter from your Company Page. This is great if you want to share company-specific information or content with your current or future clients.

To create a newsletter as a Company Page, you (or the admin of your page) must meet LinkedIn's newsletter access criteria—have Creator Mode turned on, over 150 followers or connections, a history of abiding by LinkedIn's community policies, and recently-posted original expertise-based posts and articles.

On your Company Page dashboard, find the Start a Post prompt, and click Write Article below it. This will open the publishing tool. Click Create a Newsletter, and follow the prompts from there to create and publish your newsletter.

On the right side of your Company Page dashboard, you'll see a section called Manage, which will display any events your company has scheduled, the three community hashtags that your company uses, and below that, your newsletter link and offer to sign up. You can see immediately how many subscribers you have, and you can click through to manage each of these three sections from this location.

Custom buttons

You can encourage visitors to take a particular action when they visit your Company Page by adding a custom button. This button will appear at the top of the profile under your company's logo and next to the Follow button.

On your Company Page dashboard, click the Edit Page button just to the bottom right of the cover image area. This will open a pop-up screen where you will see a list of things you can edit. Under Header, click on Buttons and you will be taken to a page where you can set this option as ON or OFF. Once you change this to ON, you will be able to create and customise. Here, you can select from five options of what you want visitors to do when they click on your button:

- Contact us
- Learn more
- Register (for an event)
- Sign up
- Visit website

Then, add the appropriate URL.

Showcase Page

A Showcase Page is an extension of your main Company Page. It is used to highlight individual brands, campaigns, departments, or initiatives in your company. A Showcase Page is useful for engaging particular audience segments and delivering specific content to them.

To create a Showcase Page, start on your Company Page dashboard. At the top right of the page, click on the Admin Tools drop-down menu, then click on Create a Showcase Page. Next, you'll be prompted to fill in some important details, starting with connecting to your existing LinkedIn Company Page. Fill in the details of your product or sub-brand, and choose a LinkedIn URL for your Showcase Page. You also have the option of uploading a logo and a short 120–character tagline to describe what you're showcasing.

Click the Create button, and you'll be taken to your Showcase Page dashboard, where you can edit your new page.

Not all companies will benefit from using Showcase Pages, particularly if they have a cohesive main target market. Showcase Pages also require their own unique content to engage followers, so consider whether the additional workload is worth it or if you would be better off focusing on your main Company Page.

Analytics

Analytics is one of the most useful features of a Company Page. Analytics help you understand your followers better, measure engagement, and optimise how you connect with your market.

You can find the Analytics menu in the top left menu bar of your Company Page's dashboard. From this menu, you can get data on these five areas:

- Visitors
- Followers
- Leads
- Updates
- Competitors

Use the data on these pages to understand your current follower base, learn more about who is visiting your page, and assess what content you post engages with your audience—and what doesn't. This will help with planning what kind of content to write in your posts and newsletters, how to find and convert new followers, and how to engage with all of your followers and visitors further.

'Example is not the main thing in influencing others; it is the only thing.' **—Albert Schweitzer**

David B. Horne

David B. Horne is the founder of Add Then Multiply, a consultancy working exclusively with business founders who want to grow fast. David trained as a chartered accountant with PwC and his career includes being CFO of two companies listed on London's Alternative Investment Market where he raised more than £100 million in funding and bought or sold more than twenty companies.

David is author of Amazon #1 bestselling *Add Then Multiply—How Small Businesses Can Think Like Big Businesses and Achieve Exponential Growth*. It sets out David's proven FACE methodology—Fund, Acquire, Consolidate, Exit—which supports rapid growth. His book won the Business Self Development category at the Australian Business Book Awards 2020.

He is also the founder of Funding Focus, an educational business that is raising awareness and supporting women and racial minorities who face a very uneven playing field when trying to raise capital for their businesses.

What was the biggest challenge you were having with LinkedIn before working with the Prominence Global team?

Connecting with the right kind of people, and at scale, without having to spend ages doing it manually.

How has your time spent on LinkedIn changed since joining the program?

All of my time on LinkedIn is now spent nurturing relationships and building my profile as a thought leader. All of the day-to-day tactical stuff (connections, endorsements, birthday messages, new job messages, etc.) is dealt with for me by the Prominence Global team, so that I can focus on the added-value stuff.

Can you share one or two benefits you have experienced since joining the program?

In just over a year, my connections have grown from 2,000 to 9,000, and my posts are regularly reaching audiences of several thousand. My record so far is more than 10,000 views of a single post.

I've also learned a lot about changes to LinkedIn as they happen, so that I can always be on the leading edge of what's going on. For example, when the LinkedIn event feature first came out, with the Prominence Global team's assistance, I was able to increase attendance at two events that I ran because we created a message campaign to my target audience.

How has this impacted you, either personally or as results for your business?

Many people have said to me that they are constantly seeing me active on LinkedIn and they ask me how I can afford to spend so much time on there. I smile, knowing that Prominence Global is my secret weapon.

David B. Horne
www.linkedin.com/in/david-b-horne
www.addthenmultiply.com
www.funding-focus.com

CHAPTER 8

A Clear Message

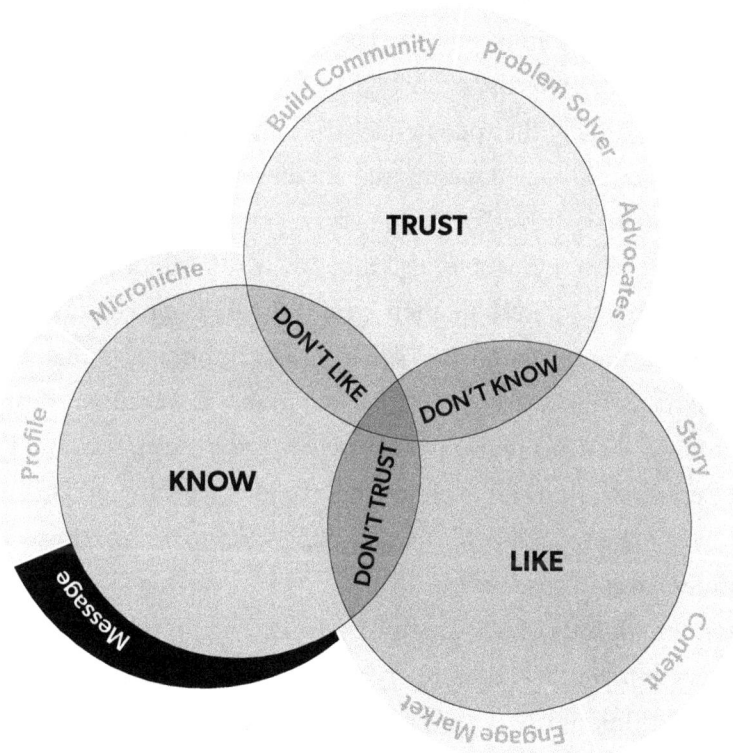

There is a final piece of the puzzle in the first phase of having people get to really know you, and this is to have a clear message about who you are and what is the value proposition you represent. Most importantly, it clarifies exactly what the problem is that you solve. There is an entire chapter on this to come, but for now it's enough to know that your profile needs to be crystal clear on this.

Once you have an excellent LinkedIn profile that tells the story of who you are, who you help, the problem you solve, and a little about how you go about that, you should have a tight niche. This will help attract the people who are most likely to be interested in you and your solutions, and the content you will soon create that showcases your expertise in this area.

It's highly likely that people will start checking out your profile and discovering your content, and increasingly they will want to access more in-depth information about your services.

I often see many people on LinkedIn who have done the hard work to create interest in their profiles, and their solutions fail spectacularly at this important step. I've lost count of how many TV commercials I've watched without being able to recall afterwards what they were promoting or even what the business was. I've met people who cannot explain what they do for a living. I'm sure you have experienced this too. You don't want to be like those TV commercials or those people.

On the flip side of this are those advertisements that try to pack in every buzzword and as many messages as possible into thirty seconds, thinking they need to get the biggest possible bang for their buck. Or that guy at the networking event who, when asked the inevitable question ('So, what do you do?') replies with a well-rehearsed response that sounds like it was written by someone else and is completely lacking in authenticity. Worse still are those people who use so much jargon or 'big' words that nobody understands what they're on about. Once again, you don't want to be one of those people.

Moving from first view to client

Your clear message is about the next step people will take when they have been through the entire journey: *know, like, trust.* There will certainly be people who will reach out to you directly through interaction with your content. They might send a direct message on your profile asking for an appointment with you, or for directions on how to find information.

This is normal activity and takes place on my profile every week. However, while this is the outcome you want, the majority of people will still want to access more detail before doing so.

This next step is your opportunity to go much deeper than your LinkedIn profile allows. Use video content and written content that walks your new visitor through a clear pathway leading to whatever the best next step is. There is a saying in marketing that I believe in very strongly:

Each marketing message you create has just one purpose: to sell the next message.

This goes back to what I alluded to previously. Many LinkedIn profiles fail spectacularly in moving people from interest to becoming a client, or from being a cold lead to a warm one and then to a client. The mistake these profiles make is in trying to sell the outcome instead of the next step.

If your product or service is worth hundreds of dollars then this step can be shorter, but if people are required to invest thousands of dollars, or make a recurring monthly investment, it is very unlikely that they will progress from having found you on LinkedIn to becoming a client in one step. Once your profile has done its job and attracted interest, your next step will be crucial in turning an abundance of warm leads into clients. Otherwise those people will simply move onto the next person who does this step better than you.

Selling the next step

And now we come to the nugget of gold in this chapter: ensure your next message sells the next step. This will vary for each individual, but that next step will probably fit into one of these five categories:

1. Webinar
2. Phone call
3. Online meeting (Skype, Zoom, etc.)
4. Face-to-face meeting
5. Any of the above with someone on your team

Work out which of these options will be the appropriate next step for you, and then craft your message around it (or brief your copywriters to do this for you).

Now that you're thinking of the 'message' as a series of logical next steps, work out how many steps you need to move people from simply viewing your profile and consuming the content to becoming clients. This is often referred to as a 'funnel'. Funnels can be quite generic in nature, so it's up to you to make yours specific, just like your niche.

To illustrate this point, I will use a campaign we recently created for one of our clients as an example.

The objective was to move people from being merely content consumers on LinkedIn to signing up for a training program at $19,000 per participant. These are the messages that took place:

1. LinkedIn content positions the CEO as highly influential in this industry to gain visibility on the profile.
2. Profile outlines the service more than the business itself.
3. Profile leads interested people to access more information about the service online.
4. A direct message leads people to attend an upcoming, free live half-day event.
5. Half-day event gives great value and invites people who want to explore the opportunity of the main program to book in for a small, group information session.
6. Small group session gives a complete outline of the program and expected outcomes, and the opportunity to sign up to the program on a payment plan over ten months.

As you can see, instead of directing people to a page that explained the program, each step simply sold the *next* step, which gave people the opportunity to move at their own pace, starting with finding our client on LinkedIn and finishing with investing $19,000.

Let's focus on just one step: moving from engaging with you on LinkedIn to choosing to seek more information elsewhere. You can direct people with some very simple next steps, using the powerful tools on LinkedIn that will help you elevate yourself above the masses, which is exactly what every good influencer does.

The first option is to direct people to your website. It's very easy to add a link to your communications and on your profile that directs people to your website. This is one of the simplest and quickest options to make more information available about your services, including information on why you created your website in the first place.

If you plan to do this, it's extremely important that your website has a clear message about the value you provide, and that it's congruent with your LinkedIn message.

When potential new clients reach out to me, the first thing we do is work out whether we are a good fit for them and vice versa. We start by looking at their website to get a better understanding of them and their services, and this tells us a lot. Often it is the case that their websites are confusing and, even worse, not aligned with their niche.

If you haven't updated your website in some time, it will be worth your while as part of this journey to do so now, taking care to ensure that you have congruency with your niche.

Alternatively, a quick fix could be to create a new page on your website that focuses entirely on your niche. Instead of directing people to your home page, you could direct them from LinkedIn to this page instead.

Either way, keep in mind that whatever people are viewing at this point, there must be a clear message, and that message should be promoting the next step you want them to take. From there, you will need to have your multi-stepped funnel in place, with a clear message for each of the subsequent steps in your customer's journey.

Hopefully, by now you are getting some real insights into the power of clear messaging, and how critical it is to the success of your influencer journey. If you don't already have them, I suggest you invest some time in building these assets as part of this journey. Keep in mind that you are investing ninety days in a process of launching yourself onto the world stage as a highly influential person in your chosen industry.

This is where a good portion of that time should be invested. You may want to park progressing further through this book until you build these assets in readiness for the next steps.

We have now come to the end of the first influence pillar, which is to get people to *know* who you are, see the value of what you bring to the table, and understand why they might want to find out more. If you have followed the process up to this point, by now you should have a world-class profile, a laser focus on your microniche, and understand the importance of that microniche. You will also have a very clear message, using exceptional resources to deliver that message in a way that very few other people are doing right now.

At this stage, you will be at the pointy end of the power users on LinkedIn.

It's now time to delve into the process of getting your growing list of followers and connections to really like everything about you and move another step through their customer journey.

'I resent the idea that people would blame the messenger for the message, rather than looking at the content of the message itself.' —**Anita Hill**

Sam Elam

Sam Elam is a high-stakes communications skills trainer and adviser for corporate and government leaders specialising in media interviews, public speaking, and presentations. Sam teaches executives and leaders the connective power of clear, confident and dynamic communication for recognition, action and influence in day-to-day leadership demands and during times of potential, reputation-damaging crisis events.

What was the biggest challenge you were having with LinkedIn before working with the Prominence Global team?
Building the right connections. I did not know how to approach targeted, industry influencers and potential clients for connection so they would want to connect and not view my approach as purely a sales request. I was not aware of the algorithms associated with LinkedIn and the best way to structure content—both volume and type.

How has your time spent on LinkedIn changed since joining the program?
I am interacting with the right influencers and potential clients in one-on-one, direct interactions. Even the most senior of C-suite executives who I would not normally have access to—unless I knew them personally—are responding. I am easily producing regular content that

is no longer random but instead is strategic, diverse and purposeful in attracting recognition and attention from the right people.

Can you share one or two benefits you have experienced since joining the program?

I now know the features of LinkedIn and understand how my page and activity need to be set up and written to rank well. I have a well-structured, easy-to-achieve content plan.

How has this impacted you, either personally or as results for your business?

I have grown my connection base by thousands of quality connections which would have taken me years to achieve through any other marketing activity. I can go to them directly to build rapport and a relationship which is the best way to develop new business. Although I am only a few months in and have not started running any campaigns or converting connections to my database, my new connections are proactively contacting me asking for our services.

Sam Elam

www.linkedin.com/in/sam-elam

www.mediamanoeuvres.com.au

CHAPTER 9

Stories and Why They Matter

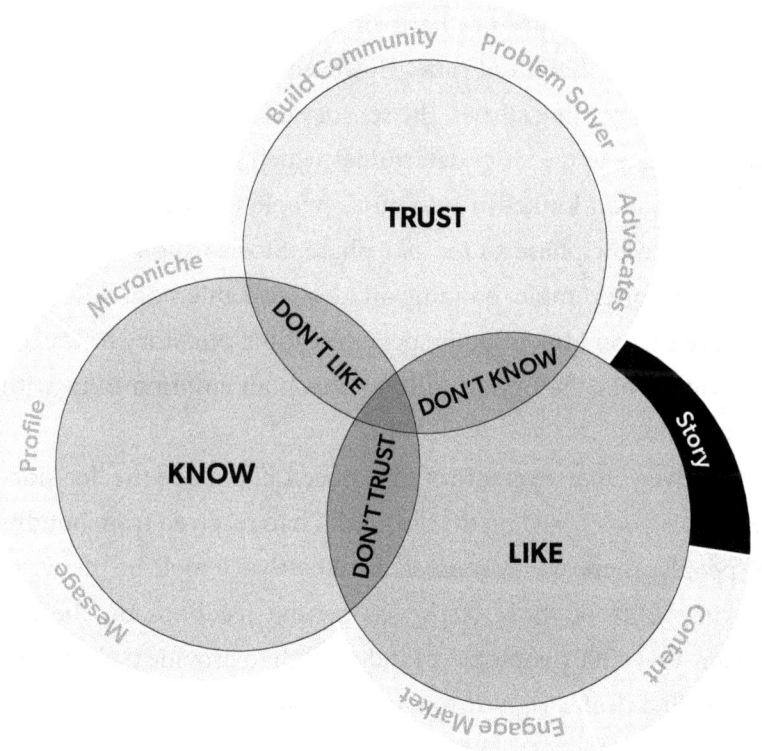

If you look back at some of the most successful ad campaigns of the past few years, most likely they were focused on telling stories.

There is actually some science behind the concept of using stories in advertising; it's not just the latest flavour-of-the-month marketing angle.

When we have to process bland content, such as our business' financial accounts, the areas of the brain that activate are known as the Broca's area and the Wernicke's area, which are named after two neuroscientists who did a lot of research into this concept. In general terms, we are not hardwired to retain this type of information for any length of time. However, when we are listening to, watching or reading stories, the sensory cortex is activated, and the way we relate to the story determines which sense is activated.

Our goal on LinkedIn is to move people through their journey, from the *know* phase to the *like* phase. Stories align a cause with an effect, for example, bonding an idea with an emotion. If we can achieve this on LinkedIn, the person reading our story or watching our videos has the opportunity to attach an emotion to us within themselves.

To give you an example of this, once I had made the decision to write this book based on the feedback I had received from hundreds of people, there was a process of steps that I took in the writing journey. One of those steps was getting feedback on the cover design. Over 200 people were kind enough to provide their thoughts on the first drafts, right through to the final version, and hopefully you will like the outcome. A number of people provided feedback, for instance: 'Having known (and enjoyed) your personality on webcasts, I don't think either of these designs bring out your personality.'

And this one: 'They are a little too complicated, which is not you. In my mind you're uncomplicated, so the covers need to outline that.'

These kind people went as far as sharing how they would be likely to attach this book, in their thoughts, to my personality (or lack thereof). In other words, the more people that have the means to get to know us, the more likely they will be to create a sense of us as we relate to them. The trick, of course, is to ensure that they relate to us in a positive way.

Keep in mind that all of our stories are intended to elicit an emotion, of which there are many. Existing research suggests that we are capable of twenty-seven different emotions:

Admiration	Adoration	Appreciation
Amusement	Anxiety	Awe
Awkwardness	Boredom	Calmness
Confusion	Craving	Desire
Disgust	Empathy	Entrancement
Envy	Excitement	Fear
Horror	Interest	Joy
Nostalgia	Romance	Sadness
Satisfaction	Sympathy	Triumph

Clearly, we probably want to steer clear of a number of these. These are the ones we most want to create in our viewers:

Admiration	Appreciation	Amusement
Awe	Craving	Excitement
Interest	Joy	Satisfaction

There are three critical stories that you need to focus on to help people make this transition from simply knowing you to liking you, and they are your story, your clients' stories, and your business' story.

Telling these stories in a way that engenders some of these nine positive emotions is a sure-fire and proven method for allowing people the opportunity to like us in a way that resonates for them.

In personal branding, we are often told to create the persona we want people to know us for. I agree with that to a large extent, but I also believe that within the framework of that personal brand, allowing our connections and followers to attach to our brand the emotions that serve them best is one of the keys to shifting from simply having a personal brand to becoming an influencer with a personal brand.

Your story

At the beginning of this book, I shared my story with you at the request of many of the people I reached out to for feedback on the type of book I was thinking of writing. It was one of those eat-your-own-dog-food moments for me.

Think about that. It means that telling our stories is the logical way to get people to like us, if for no other reason than it gives insight into who we are, and what interests or motivates them to seek us out online or in person. There are a number of ways that we can share our stories, both in the sense of how we deliver them—written word, audio files such as podcasts, videos—and in the context in which they are delivered.

I suggest that all three of these mediums are important because people tend to absorb information in preferred ways. For me, it is the written word. If I want to retain information, I will always seek the written version. My wife, Julie, much prefers a visual version, with images or video. Audio books are growing in popularity since many people seem to prefer these to the written word these days (more on this in a later chapter).

I should make it clear that I'm not talking about a one-off piece of content, whether it's a video or written version of your life story. That's one piece of the story, and an important one, for sure. I strongly encourage you to create that content piece in as much detail as you're comfortable sharing. However, the most important point is that these stories are ongoing and take a number of forms. Here is a list of different approaches to your story (we go into this in more depth in a later chapter):

- Recap
- Rant
- Journey
- Learning
- Struggle
- Defining moments

Your personal and ongoing story is your opportunity to create a real connection with people on a deeper level in the online sense. Make this a part of your journey to influence and you'll be well on your way to giving people the opportunity to like you. In so doing, you'll be opening up the possibility for them to take another step through their journey with you.

Your clients' stories

Almost as important as your own story are the stories of your clients. People reading such a story will often be able to relate to that person. This will help your connections take the step from *like* to *trust*. It will also help to get a transition from followers to connections, which will again deepen that LinkedIn relationship. We all want followers, but we all value connections over followers.

There are two powerful ways you can use your clients' stories.

Case study of a client: Case studies show results, but they also are an amazing way to humanise your product or service (I have included a number of these throughout this book). This is the difference between a narrative that explains the features and benefits of your unique and remarkable solutions, and giving future or potential clients the opportunity to visualise those outcomes for themselves.

Hopefully, somewhere amongst your case studies will be a real person who has enough in common with a potential client for them to feel the excitement of imagining that a similar thing might just be in their future, too. I'm sure it goes without saying that you will need your client's permission to create a case study on them and share it on your website or in any other form of promotion.

A client's journey with you: The second way you can use a client's story is to write about their journey with you from your perspective. In this instance, you might not necessarily name the client you are referring to. The idea is to portray something that working together created for them, for instance, it could be a client they secured using your methodology, or an industry award they won, or any other positive outcome that was created by working together.

This could take the form of a written post you create, where you would focus on the story of the journey that was responsible for the outcome.

Another powerful option would be to interview your client and really showcase them—more so than yourself. This is best done through video or audio content, and the outcome of this story, in whatever form it takes, would be to make it relatable to other people, enabling them to make the connection between themselves and the outcome your current client was able to achieve with your help.

Your business' story

At some point, people will be ready to go a little deeper in their journey as your client, and at this stage they will probably want more information about your business' story before being ready to look closely at your products and services. They will probably have already been exposed to your story, and have some sense of who you are and why you matter in their world. They have probably also seen, read or heard some client stories, and made the connection between someone else and themselves.

Getting some insight into your business, your team and what you stand for beyond profits will now be of interest to them, and it's important that they not only like you but also like what your business is about. Sharing your business' *why* is what I am referring to here. This is very different to your personal *why*, which explains why you get up every day and do what you do. Your business *why* is more about the reasons for your business' existence, the problem in the world your business is here to solve, and how the world is a better place because of it.

We have a page on our website that we refer to as the 'impact page': www.prominence.global/impact. Interestingly, our analytics show that it's one of the most viewed pages on our site. Our *why* is on this page and as you will see it simply states: 'At Prominence Global we believe real and meaningful change comes through the world's entrepreneurs; people just like you. Our purpose is to help you create a powerful online presence that grows and accelerates your global footprint, so that together we really can make a huge impact.'

On the rest of the page, we share our passion for creating important impacts in the world through our partnership with the global giving movement, B1G1. The story we regularly tell is about our driving force towards our goals for those impacts. For some time that goal was to achieve one million impacts, and I'm proud to share with you that we have well and truly exceeded that goal and are now shooting for twelve million impacts as our next goal.

We share the story of how our clients are responsible for creating these impacts and how every service we offer is aligned with specific impacts that are created, such as providing food, medicines, clean drinking water, education, and many more life-changing services for people in need around the world. These stories probably create two of the most powerful emotions in people: joy and appreciation.

If you don't yet have a purpose beyond profit, however, now might be the time to consider what resonates with you and your team in creating your business *why*. If you'd like more information about B1G1, go to their website.[16] Or if you would like a personal introduction to their team just drop us an email at: admin@prominence.global. We will be more than happy to do that for you.

Your business may already have a purpose for existing or, more importantly, a purpose beyond just profit. (Let me be really clear: I have nothing against profit. Every business has a responsibility to be profitable, and, where applicable, every business owner has a responsibility to provide a comfortable and rewarding way of life for their family.)

Either way, make sure to showcase your business' *why* in your stories, and, just like with the previous two story options, this will be an ongoing sharing of these stories. It is a journey as much as it is about a dedicated page on your website or marketing statement.

---

16 www.B1G1.com

Your business' *why* doesn't have to be about charitable giving; it can be about anything you choose. There are only two critical steps you need adhere to: ensure that you have a *why*, and regularly share your *why* in your stories.

'The shortest distance between truth and a human being is a story.' **—Anthony de Mello**

David Azar

David has extensive experience managing businesses in highly competitive environments and a thorough understanding of delivering quality outcomes for clientele in large multinationals. His entrepreneurial spirit has led to his involvement in new and disruptive business opportunities, particularly those which produce positive outcomes for clients and a more sustainable future. He has an eye for doing things differently to drive profits and is passionate about innovation and its effects on sustainability, both socially and environmentally. David works with commercial property owners and managers to implement AI technology to reduce costs, increase shareholder returns, improve sustainability and elevate the tenant experience.

What was the biggest challenge you were having with LinkedIn before working with the Prominence Global team?

Understanding how to get value from it; by that I mean, a high return on time invested in engaging with the platform.

How has your time spent on LinkedIn changed since joining the program?

My time and effort are focused, structured and committed to getting a high return on investment. Previously my activity on LinkedIn was inconsistent, disorderly and without a strategic objective.

Can you share one or two benefits you have experienced since joining the program?

I am receiving far more visibility in the marketplace, therefore generating leads and conversations with people within the market who I care about. I now have clear strategic objectives around marketing and social serving within this channel. Joining the program has opened up a new way to approach the market and provided a platform to deliver this in a differentiated way.

How has this impacted you, either personally or as results for your business?

Personally, it helped inspire and motivate me on the marketing journey using digital which previously was hard to understand and navigate a path forward. For business, it has enabled me to efficiently push out a consistent and persistent message to potential and existing customers which will give me leverage and scale over time.

David Azar

www.linkedin.com/in/davidjazar

www.linkedin.com/company/adoptai

www.adopt-ai.com.au

CHAPTER 10

Know-How vs No-How

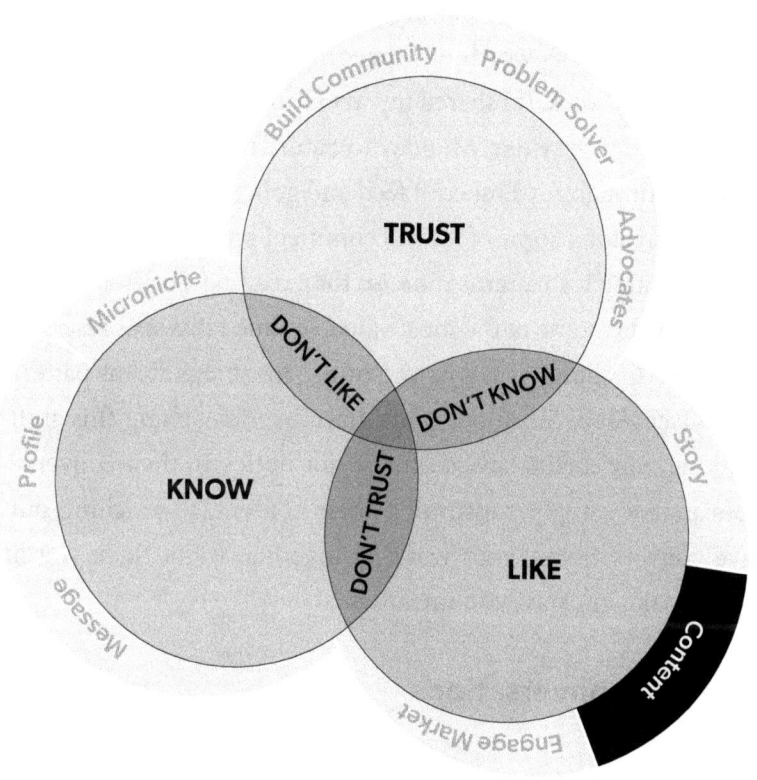

By now hopefully you are getting the gist that content is the fundamental driver of your influence, and that you need to be the author of that content. Sharing other people's content might get you some visibility online but with each post you share, you transfer the influence from you to the author of that content.

Having created literally thousands of pieces of content now for ourselves and our clients, we've tested, measured, tweaked, thrown out and hit the proverbial jackpot more times than I can now recall. I'm also a prolific consumer of content. I do read books often, but I consume a book's worth of LinkedIn content from other content creators every week. If I shared my weekly planner with you, you'd see time set aside every day, Monday to Saturday, to simply spend time scrolling through my LinkedIn feed and going to the feeds of a select group of creators. Some of it I will comment on and a lot I do not. I'm always looking for patterns more so than reading stories and articles. I consider this some of the most valuable time I invest as research.

I'd like to share with you one of the most significant patterns I have discovered. Since our team have been coaching this shift in thinking, our clients have seen a major uptick in their conversions from people simply consuming their content, to reaching out to have conversations about working together. Right there is a little clue for you, but stay with me.

Creating conversations

Here's the first of two changes you need to make to your content strategy that will make a massive difference as soon as you do so.

Once you see this, you can't unsee it. Read this section then put this book down and go scrolling through your LinkedIn feed for ten minutes and you'll see what I mean.

It's quite a simple shift and I can change your entire strategy with just seven words.

End Every Post With a Topical Question.

Sounds too simple to be true, doesn't it? However, I guarantee you if you make this change to your content, you are going to be skyrocketing up the Pyramid of Players at a rapid rate. While *what* you need to do is very simple, why is equally important.

There are three reasons why you need to make this change. The first is that this is the type of content LinkedIn prefers and is more likely to open up to wider audiences for you. They want content that keeps people on the platform, and they want content that creates conversation. In a recent announcement from LinkedIn about what gets shown in your feed, it was suggested that the more valuable a post is deemed to be, the higher up in your feed it is likely to be positioned. The first order of priority will be the content from your connections that meets these criteria.

Given that conversations are going to be considered more valuable, how do you best start a conversation? Ask a question!

The second reason to focus on content that asks questions is also given within the announcement above: *people you know*. What this means is that your content is most likely, initially at least, to be seen by the people you are connected to. If you are connecting strategically and engaging in conversations with these people, they know who you are and are likely to be interested in what you have to say, provided you keep the conversation on topic.

The third reason to use topical question-based content is when you ask a question and people answer, it positions you as the credible authority. And that is what this is all about: positioning yourself as the industry authority.

The mistake 95 percent of content creators make

I've spoken on this subject many times in presentations and in response, audiences usually have a profound realisation, so I wanted to share it here with you.

The biggest mistake I see on a daily basis when I'm spending that time scrolling through my feed is content that solves your audience's problems.

Many content creators become addicted to the admiration of their audience and want to keep giving more in the belief this engagement from their audience is proof of what they are doing works. This is the difference between 'Know-How' content and what we like to refer to as 'No-How' content.

Know-How: This type of content is exactly as it says on the box— you are sharing your expertise and solving people's problems. No wonder they love and adore you and keep coming back for more! You have positioned yourself as the authority of free advice.

No-How: This is the holy grail of content. Instead of educating your audience for free, you are educating them to understand that they have a problem they are potentially not aware they have and that you 'Know-How' to solve those problems and are the go-to person in your industry for those solutions.

We've all heard the gurus who say you should share your best content openly and as often as possible. People pay for implementation these days because there is so much free information available.

I agree as long as you are very strategic in how you frame that free information. So let's wrap this one up in a very simple framework that once again puts you further up the pyramid and in the top echelon of influencers who actually get tangible results.

1. End every post with a question
2. Educate from the view that you are highly knowledgeable in your field of expertise
3. Show you 'Know-How' to solve the problem and the solution is to get in touch with you

'There is a certain amount of dissatisfaction that goes with knowing your time, talent and abilities are not being properly used.' **—Zig Ziglar**

Daniela Grendene

Daniela is a business and executive coach with the purpose to develop strong, sustainable businesses. She works with directors, managing directors, business owners and entrepreneurs of international privately owned small- and medium-size organisations in all sectors.

What was the biggest challenge you were having with LinkedIn before working with the Prominence Global team?

My network was limited to less than 400 connections and I did not know how to expand that in a way which was genuine. I sincerely wanted to build new relationships but did not know how. My profile also read more like a CV so it did not say that much about myself.

How has your time spent on LinkedIn changed since joining the program?

I now spend about forty-five minutes to one hour every other day on LinkedIn. It's a source of valuable business information as well as a platform on which to have short business conversations which build relationships and trust.

Can you share one or two benefits you have experienced since joining the program?

Apart from the fact that my network has expanded to over 3,000 connections, I have learned how to create and share content which represents value to the audience. What I particularly like is that it is done very professionally and ethically. With the team at Prominence Global, I feel I am always a step ahead with what's changing in the world of LinkedIn.

How has this impacted you, either personally or as results for your business?

On a personal and professional level, I have very much benefitted from being part of the Prominence Global community. The sessions with Adam are always very practical but we all learn from one another, as well as from the invited guests. In addition, as a result of my presence, people have been contacting me to use my services because they feel they already know me.

Daniela Grendene
www.linkedin.com/in/daniela-grendene
www.danielagrendene.com

CHAPTER 11

Engagement the Influencer Way

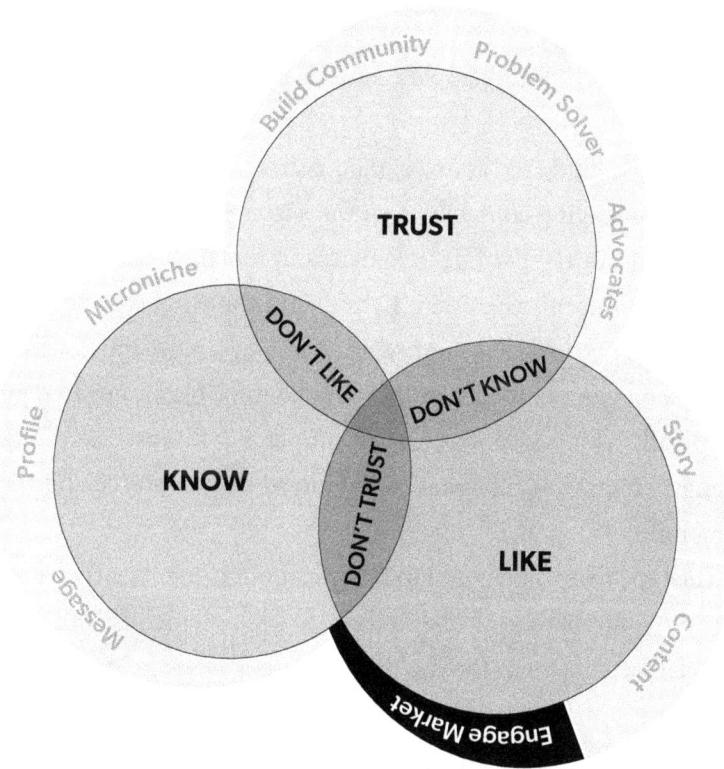

Engagement. It's almost a buzzword itself in social media these days; everyone is talking about the importance of engagement on your content. I just did a Google search using the words 'How do I get engagement on my social media content' and it returned 678 million results, containing all the usual stuff:

- Make your posts visual
- Create surveys
- Add hashtags
- Run contests
- Engage on other people's content

You will also find free courses, paid courses, platforms that create so-called 'engaging content', seven ways to this, ten ways to that, the top 100 this, thirty-five effective that, and much more.

Some of this information is helpful and some not so much. Now, don't get me wrong, I'm not trying to downplay the importance of having engaging content (in the next chapter this is covered very specifically as it relates to creating influence). It's just not the type of engagement I'm referring to as one of the nine accelerators of influence.

The type of engagement I'm talking about is the type that almost nobody who perceives themselves as social media influencers creates (see chapter 2 for the difference between 'influencers' and 'influential'), which is to engage with the comments or points of view that people leave on your content.

Responding to followers

I was listening to a talkback radio show in my car on the way to the beach yesterday, and one of the show hosts referred to a celebrity who actually responds to many of the comments left by his fans on his social media profiles. The host seemed to be in awe of the fact that he did this, and pointed out how rare it is for celebrities to engage in the way this person did, and how it set him apart.

One level down from celebrities are the influencers, who may just be well known on one particular platform such as YouTube or Instagram, and are generating income and/or free products through their profiles. More often than not, these people rarely engage with those who are giving them the opportunity to have their piece of fame. When you go onto their profiles and look through their content, what you see are one-sided interactions. In fairness to some, the amount of commentary required is often huge and it would be difficult for them to reply to every comment; many of the better-paid ones employ people to respond as them on their behalf.

My point here is that our type of influencer *does* respond to the comments left by people on their content on LinkedIn, and to the direct messages that people send (with the exception of spam comments and messages, of course). This is by far one of the major differences that set these influencers apart, placing them in the previously mentioned 0.02 percent of people on LinkedIn.

The reality is that you're not talking about or realistically attempting to have thousands of comments on your content. You are niching in fields of expertise, and therefore appealing to a laser-focused group of people, not the masses of a celebrity endorsement or general social media.

Yes, I have had, and many of my clients have had, individual pieces of content generate hundreds of thousands of views on our content and profiles, plus thousands of likes and comments. For me personally, my most successful content piece generated in excess of 500,000 views, more than 200,000 comments and 75,000 searches on my profile in one week. These are the exceptions and not the rule, and sometimes this is what we are actively attempting to achieve. However, in the normal course of any given content piece's lifespan, it will generate views in the thousands, or occasionally 10,000 plus. Twenty to 100 comments per post is ideal, with anything above that a welcome bonus. At these levels, it's possible and realistic to respond to the people who have taken the time to engage with our content.

So, in very simple terms, 'engagement' as a driver of influence is how *you* engage with people, more so than the standard definition of engagement in general social media terms. If you're not prepared to interact with people on your content, and in the more private realm of direct messages, you will struggle to position yourself as the go-to person in your industry.

Is it okay to have your team respond as you? Yes, although I personally attempt to respond as the public face of engagement on my content. In 90 percent of occasions, it will be me responding, allowing for the fact that I am often on planes, in different time zones, or speaking at live events. On these occasions, I don't change the timing of my content, and in fact I stick to a quite regimented posting schedule (this is covered in the next chapter). At times like this, one of my team will respond on my behalf.

The same goes for direct messages. I do this as often as possible myself, and the team keeps the momentum and response times within our guidelines when I cannot. Since I know when my content is being shared in advance, I do make time in my schedule each day for this task; I consider this one of the most important tasks I do every day.

Do some people I know fully outsource this? Yes, they do. Do they still achieve great results? Yes, they do, but only after briefing their teams extremely well on how to go about this.

How you structure this task to fit within your daily schedule is entirely up to you, although I suggest that if it's possible, you do most of it personally. This will give you the best long-term results.

How you or your team respond is also a big driver of your personal brand, which we touched on previously. This is likely to be the most public, potentially scrutinised, and, at times, criticised part of your journey to influence.

Handling negative feedback

Many people I have coached have gone along for months getting great traction with their content, following best practice, and then they receive that inevitable piece of negative feedback, either about their point of view on a post or, more importantly, on a response they have made to someone else, who has then commented on their content. Suddenly it seems as though their world has been shattered;

someone does not agree and is quite vocal in their opinion of the subject matter.

Personally, I would celebrate this event if I were you—99 percent of the time it will not be the end of the world as you know it. You won't need to move to a deserted island to let the dust settle. What it does mean is that you have started to become known for your point of view on your topic of expertise and have discovered that not everyone agrees with you. This will be covered in more depth in a later chapter, but for now I will simply say that you should accept that you will get opposing opinions.

You will also get competitors looking to ride your coat tails of increasing influence, and on some occasions you will attract the haters. In Australia, we use the term 'tall poppy syndrome' to describe the tendency to discredit or disparage someone else who has achieved wealth or prominence in public life. While this term is generally aimed at people in public office, or who have high status in business circles, or celebrities, it's also commonly used in all forms of social media. Social media gives the haters a public forum to do what they do. The haters are best ignored; they will move on soon enough.

How you handle the people who have a legitimately different point of view, or call you out when you make a mistake, is again what puts you in our 0.02-percent club. You should respond with complete honesty. If you firmly believe in your point of view—and you should, or you shouldn't have shared it in the first place—then justify your opinion. If you feel that the other person's point of view has some validity, acknowledge that fact.

Sometimes other people in my field don't agree with some

aspects of my personal opinions on certain topics. I realise this, so when I express these opinions I will often add a caveat such as: 'This is my personal belief; however, I acknowledge that there are other credible experts in this field who do not agree.'

A simple statement like this, if you know there's a possibility of differing opinions, will negate a high number of challenges to your point of view. It will also give you the ability to respond by agreeing that there can be more than one opinion on the subject matter.

If you find yourself dealing with somebody who chooses to disagree, you can agree to disagree, or you can further validate your opinion with more insights based on your experience. Engaging in debate on a subject you raise is one of the best outcomes you can achieve and is one of the best opportunities you will be gifted with for deepening your influence. However, my caveat to that is: 'As long as you can back it up.'

Dealing with competitors

When it comes to dealing with competitors, well, this is one of those topics where many people with expert opinions may not agree with me. This is my personal belief and I acknowledge that other credible experts in this field may not agree with me.

I believe there is an abundance of everything we desire or need in this world. I am also a believer in the process I'm sharing here, and its power to set you apart from the majority of your competitors. Their attempt to ride your coat tails is flattering. If you agree, then there is nothing you need to do differently. If you don't agree and would like a strategy to ensure this does not happen, here it is.

Make a list of people you believe are competitors, or people you would not want engaging on your content. It doesn't matter if you're connected or not on LinkedIn right now. Go to their profile on LinkedIn and click on the More tab, which is in the top section of their profile below their profile picture and headline. One of the options in the drop-down menu is Report/Block. Select this, and then select Block. Blocking someone will prevent them from viewing your profile or your connections. It will also remove their ability to see or engage with your content. If you are first-degree connections, LinkedIn will remove them as such. Problem solved.

As your influence increases, so too, potentially, will you find more people you want to add to this blocked status, so just block them as and when you see fit. Definitely use this strategy for bona fide haters when you encounter them.

To sum up, the engagement you have with your followers, and those who respond to your content, is the holy grail of engagement in your journey of influence. Yes, of course you want and need the standard definitions of engagement, but it's how you respond in all situations—the different opinions and the haters—that will set you above the pack. You will be unlikely to maintain a position as an influential person in your industry if you're not willing to engage in this manner.

'The more you engage and connect, the more engagements and connections you will have.' —**Loren Wiseman**

Jason Tan

Jason Tan is the director of Data Driven Analytics. Together with his team, he helps insurance companies increase profit per unit of economics through embedding and automating analytics into the business front line. Jason also hosts *The Analytics Show* podcast, where he interviews business leaders around the world about building and running a modern high-performing organisation using data and analytics.

What was the biggest challenge you were having with LinkedIn before working with the Prominence Global team?

I would say not knowing where and how to start with my LinkedIn profile. While I understood what the platform could do for my business, I didn't have any overarching strategy to use the platform for my business and podcast.

How has your time spent on LinkedIn changed since joining the program?

I now have a clear strategy and also a framework to follow in building my authority on LinkedIn. I no longer wake up in the morning just to decide what to do on LinkedIn; instead, I have the strategy and work planned out for the entire month that helps me to build authority and relationships with key stakeholders on LinkedIn.

Can you share one or two benefits you have experienced since joining the program?

I built *The Analytics Show* podcast from the ground up to where it is today. The only platform I use and rely on to build the podcast is LinkedIn and I do this by applying the strategy I learned from Adam.

How has this impacted you, either personally or as results for your business?

I am now known as a data analytics expert within my own circle of connections and followers. Not only can I easily pitch high-profile guests through my LinkedIn profile, more than that, I have people reaching out to me for business and partnerships.

Jason Tan

www.linkedin.com/in/jpctan

www.linkedin.com/company/ddalabs

ddalabs.ai

CHAPTER 12

The Content Plan

'Stop writing about everything. So many brands create content and try to cover everything, instead of focusing on the core niche that they can position themselves as an expert around. No one cares about your special recipe ... Find your niche, and then go even more niche.' —**Joe Pulizzi**

If engagement was not a big eye-opener for you, then content probably will be. In fact, it could be argued that this chapter should have preceded engagement, given that my definition of engagement relates mostly to your content. I'm reminded right now of that question, 'Which came first, the chicken or the egg?' To me it doesn't matter because I love chicken and eggs equally, and it's a similar distinction here as to which should come first. My reason for putting engagement first is so you have a deeper understanding of the need to create content, and why the type of content you create is so important.

Either way, strap in and grab your notebook if you haven't

already. This is one of the longest chapters of this book. If you've been powering through and are close to needing a break, take it now and come back when you're refreshed.

This chapter highlights where the majority of people go wrong on LinkedIn, in general and also on the journey to becoming highly influential. Sharing the wrong content can destroy your personal brand in a similar way to not engaging with your community, so before we dive into an effective content strategy, let's start with my five guidelines for things to be aware of and possibly avoid.

1. **LinkedIn is not Facebook or Instagram.** You are looking to create a personal brand using LinkedIn as your chosen platform. It is not the place to share your social life and the latest things going on with your family and friends. There's nothing wrong with doing that, but it's not appropriate to do it on LinkedIn. If you want to know about those kinds of things going on in my world, by all means connect with me on Facebook or Instagram. You're very welcome to see that side of my life. Even our cat has his own Instagram page, with a few thousand followers.

2. **Too much content.** Influence is not generated through quantity of content on LinkedIn; it comes through quality content. You don't need to treat your LinkedIn profile like Twitter and share content every hour of the day. The more content you share on LinkedIn, the less likely you will be to gain traction. This is due to the way the algorithms deal with content shown

in feeds, and the suppression of what is deemed low-quality tactics, or spam content.

3. **Spamming groups.** I've seen so many so-called LinkedIn strategies that suggest you should join as many groups as possible (you can join 100 in total), and push out as many links to your blog posts and latest offers that you can. On the flip side, I see many people complaining that groups on LinkedIn don't get anywhere near the traction that other platforms achieve. Ask yourself if you really want to spend your precious time looking over endless pitches by group members. Or is your reason for choosing to join a group more about community, and having a place to learn and interact with other like-minded people? Influential people are active in groups; they are not active in this manner.

4. **Self-promotion.** By all means promote yourself and what it is you do, but be aware that there is an acceptable limit on how much you do this. You will soon encounter my thirteen-point content plan, but here's a heads-up. Only two out of every thirteen pieces of content will be self-promotional.

Think of the last party or networking event you attended. Who was the person everyone talked about but did not enjoy talking to? It was probably the person who never stopped talking about themselves. In real life, we don't warm to people who do this, and we don't tolerate it online either. As you become more influential, more and more people will want to know your story and what you have to say; they just don't want every piece of content you share to be about you.

5. **Curated content.** You'll recall that I stated previously that there are times when I will share my point of view and add the caveat explaining that it's my personal belief and I acknowledge that there are other credible experts in this field who do not agree with me. Well, this is another personal point of view.

I see lots of strategies suggesting that creating influence is simple. All you need to do is find articles written by other experts and share them with your community, suggesting that, in your opinion, it's worth them taking the time to read them. You might think this is a more effective strategy than taking the time to create your own quality content. I respectfully disagree. In my opinion, it's far better to be the person others refer to, and whose content and opinions others share.

I'm not suggesting that there isn't a place for sharing other people's content, but I do question the wisdom of an entire strategy revolving around curated content.

From here on in the book I will use the word 'community' a great deal; in fact, the very next chapter is dedicated to the individuals that make up your community. These are the people who believe what you believe: they follow you or connect with you, and most importantly they regularly engage with your content (more about these very special people in the next chapter).

Now that you know what you *shouldn't* be doing, it's time to get clear on what you *should* be doing as it relates to your content strategy. There are four steps for you to implement.

Step 1: The right content

Just as there are certain things you should not do in your content strategy, equally there are specific content types you should focus on:

Text-only status updates

These posts, which will show up in your connections and followers feeds, are short-form bite-sized pieces of content. Although they are short in word count, they can pack a big punch. They often have the ability to create the most engagement when you share your expertise regularly. Keep in mind that more and more people are consuming content via their phones these days, so short-form content that is well written and targeted to your niche is likely to be favourably received by your community.

Text with images

These are the same as your text-only posts, with the addition of an image or images. If you were writing a blog post or creating a new web page, you would likely spend a lot of time and energy on making sure you add the right images. Interestingly, I find that content with images gets less traction on LinkedIn than just text-based content. My tips regarding image selection are to keep it relevant to the subject matter, and also avoid the overuse of stock images. Screenshots or real-life images often seem to work best.

Native video

Video has the potential to be the holy grail of content; however, on LinkedIn there are a few guidelines to follow to get the best traction for your videos.

- Videos should always be 'native upload', which means that you upload the video file directly onto the platform, either via your desktop or your phone. Avoid using YouTube or Vimeo links; videos loaded directly onto LinkedIn will always get better reach than links to other platforms.
- Videos should be kept to under two minutes in length. If a video runs beyond this, people will be much less likely to watch it, or at least watch it to the end. Just like your short-form, text-based status-update posts, videos are usually watched on phones, and the better you are at creating punchy, information-rich content, the more likely you are to attract your community.
- Captions are a must. Most video content—in fact, over 85 percent—is watched without sound. This is not specific to LinkedIn, but it is as relevant to LinkedIn as it is to all other platforms. It does take more effort to create video content with captions, but if you don't use them, the majority of your videos, and the message they contain, will be missed.

Curated content

Yes, there is a place for this type of content in your strategy, but it is well below the above three content types in importance, so use it sparingly. When appropriate, ensure that you tag the original author in your post on LinkedIn and give your opinion as to why you believe this is content worth reading for your community. I believe that the best-curated content you can use is that which already exists on LinkedIn; you can simply share a status post, native video or article that your chosen author has already uploaded recently. Sharing external links to any form of content, such as blog articles, YouTube videos and landing pages, is something that tends to be suppressed in feeds.

As your feeds get busier, LinkedIn will attempt to keep what you see on the platform itself. I believe that more social platforms will take this approach in the future, which is why curated content is having less traction as a strategy in itself. It does and will have relevance, however, if you only share relevant posts that don't use external links and were authored directly on LinkedIn.

Articles

LinkedIn gives you your own blogging platform as part of your personal profile. Articles are long-form, in-depth posts with a character limit of around 100,000 characters. In years gone by, this was where LinkedIn placed most of the emphasis on sharing content into feeds. However, recent changes to LinkedIn's algorithms mean that articles are no longer able to gain the traction they once did. Now, the preferred option is to focus on newsletters.

Newsletters

Newsletters were once only available to very few select LinkedIn members, but as of late 2021, access to this content type became available to all users who had turned on Creator Mode and met a few basic criteria—having over 150 followers or connections, a history of abiding by LinkedIn's community policies, and recently-posted original expertise-based posts and articles.

The option to create newsletters is particularly useful if you are a regular writer of articles and want even more engagement with followers and to build a subscription platform. LinkedIn newsletters are a type of long-form content, with a character limit of over 100,000. You can use newsletters to talk about a professional topic you're passionate about on a regular basis, and demonstrate your depth of knowledge to your community. LinkedIn members can subscribe to your newsletter to be notified about new newsletters you publish, allowing you to build and grow a regularly engaged audience.

LinkedIn makes it easy to invite followers or connections to subscribe, and you can promote your newsletter using push notifications, in-app and emails which are sent to all your subscribers. You can simplify the building of your subscriber base by making your newsletter easily searchable for all LinkedIn members to discover, read and share. You'll also be able to see the name and profile of those who subscribe, even if they are not already connected to or following you.

Feedback and comments from readers are easy to obtain through newsletters, and LinkedIn analytics will indicate readership and shareability.

Polls

You now have the option to include short polls as content. They can be a great option for gaining insights via the opinions of LinkedIn members. Polls allow up to four pre-defined responses to a question you pose. One of the features I like most about polls is as the creator of the poll, you can view who votes for each option. If you use your polls as a strategic way to gather intel, you can connect with or communicate with each individual based on the answer they chose.

I do see many people creating what I would suggest are somewhat pointless polls, simply designed to elicit a response. I'd highly recommend using polls that ask questions of value or allow you to continue conversations in a professional manner.

Documents

This option allows you to create a post that includes a downloadable document. There is no end of options as to what may be of value to your audience, and of course it will vary industry by industry. Remember that posts that are more likely to get the best traction are status posts and they are limited to just 3,000 characters, which will be around 500 words on average. Documents can be up to 300 pages long or 100 megabytes in size. Having the option to include something with more information is potentially a way to use the initial written post to garner interest, while allowing the document to go deeper on the subject.

Some options to consider are:

- PowerPoint-style presentations
- Instructional manuals
- Brochures
- Invites

Step 2: The content plan

We have used this exact framework—the thirteen-point content plan—with over 500 clients with great success, and I'm going to make it really simple for you to create your own content plan. If you follow this advice exactly, your content will be compliant with LinkedIn's preferences, you will have the perfect amount of content without overdoing it and having some of your content suppressed, and you will have a simple process that is easy to replicate and follow month after month.

I suggest you include the following in your monthly content plan:

- Long-form newsletter articles
- Polls
- Status posts with images
- Status posts with no images
- Status posts with a link
- Status post with a document
- Native videos
- Native videos with a link

These posts should be a mixture of content that your community would want to consume and content that positions you as highly influential in your industry without seeming too 'salesy'. I recommend that you divide the posts into four categories:

Interesting

Your stories will cross all categories. Hopefully, it's obvious that your stories could easily fall into the interesting category; however, they are not the only type of content that does. Those in your community will also have opinions, so one of the most interesting content pieces could be where you start the conversation and allow your community, through the comments, to share theirs. Of course, this will vary immensely from industry to industry, and possibly country to country.

A good post will pose a point of view and allow your community to weigh in with their thoughts; this creates the engagement I referred to in the last chapter and gives your community a voice to be heard.

Industry

Your content should also be about your industry; you need to show that you're at the cutting edge of your field of expertise. If there's breaking news or some form of change in the status quo, by forming an opinion or simplifying the complicated you're showing that you care enough to keep your community updated, or making what is likely common knowledge easier to understand.

While you will need to create your status posts or videos, there will be a plethora of industry bodies, podcasts, groups or news articles about every facet of your industry. All you need to do is subscribe to any of your preferred options and your content will almost create itself, which means that you need to do very little research into the subject matter. The key is to have an opinion for or against, and phrase it as a question so your community can share their opinions, too. The topic might be well known, but you are now the industry expert because you asked the question.

I'll use a post of mine as an example:

It feels like a lot of my LinkedIn connections are speakers. But did you know glossophobia, or fear of public speaking, is so widely feared that it's considered a worse fate than death?!

I also love delivering keynotes. But it is a funny realisation that we speakers are in fact the outliers, that the world at large, outside my tiny world, is really afraid of speaking.

It seems I've unwittingly become part of a 'speaker bubble', where a lot of my connections like to speak, and so I see more and more of it. So now I'm trying to pop it, not only to keep me sane, but also to see if there are any LinkedIn users who are comfortable saying they don't get fired up by the opportunity to speak.

So tell me, what's your view on speaking? Does it petrify you, or do you live for the stage?

Short and to the point—just eight sentences in total—but it packed a punch for plenty of people who had an opinion to share.

Promotional

Of course, we all want to be able to promote our events, services, special offers, etc. There's no point in being active on social media if it doesn't lead to revenue generation of some description. So, yes, you can and should create promotional content, but it should only be to promote that next step we have spoken about. In my opinion this is a rookie mistake I see daily on LinkedIn: in most cases people go in for the kill, so to speak, too early.

When it's appropriate to create this type of content, make sure you have built your funnel, and create your promotional content to move people to the next step in their buyer's journey. As we have already discussed, this could be to come to your webinar, or your free event, or to have an online meeting where you will be providing some great value.

I have only used written posts as examples in this section; these posts can, and at times should, be video content.

Not all that long ago, a connection posted a great promotional video that used both written and video content, and was really getting some traction. This was the written content that accompanied that video:

[FREE GIFT]

I've been applying the Key Person of Influence methodology for a few years now and seen amazing results, so I've teamed up with them to offer you a couple free gifts!
They have a proven five-step process that just works.

They've helped hundreds of businesses stand out and scale up, and they've donated more than $4 million through charitable giving.

So I reached out to the Dent team and asked if there's anything we could do to pass on some value to you.

We've come up with two free gifts:

The Influence Score Card: This free forty-question test benchmarks your ability to influence in a business or leadership context and identifies opportunities for leveraged growth.

And the Key Person of Influence book shows you how to use the 5Ps methodology to become more visible, valuable, and connected in your industry.

Grab them from the links below (no strings attached).

I'm sure you're thinking, that's great, Adam, but how does it help me? A promotion like this has the potential to be very powerful on many levels. Still using the same example, let me outline a few of the advantages for me from this connection:

- I am now in the position of being highly influential; I have partnered with a world-class business Dent (www.dent. global).
- My community receives valuable and free content through Dent's scorecard and book, and the best part is that I didn't have to create any of the content (other than the post and video).
- Dent will reciprocate the favour by promoting something of mine at a later date that is also free.

- Both Dent and I benefit because the suggestion to take up the free offer is by someone else rather than ourselves, and we both get to expose in an appropriate way the first step in our funnels to a new audience. We've added value to our respective communities to mutual benefit.

You can also do the standard promotion where you simply offer your own next step in the funnel, a concept that I'm sure doesn't require any in-depth explanation.

The rant

Ah, the rant, one of my favourite content strategies. If there's anything that gets the opinions flowing, it's a good rant. I'm sure you're all familiar with the rant. Briefly, it's a tirade or venting of frustration. It's you on your soapbox telling the world you're sick of seeing something occur.

A WORD OF WARNING: Use the rant sparingly or you risk being seen as a whinger. You might get a few comments to this effect on each post, and for now just take my word for it that this is quite okay (I will explain why in more detail in the next chapter).

In my opinion, the best way of using a rant is to combine it with a promotional objective, although it's more than acceptable to just simply use it to allow your community their voice. The key is not just to rant but to also offer a solution. This will move you from being a potential whinger to the person with the answers: the industry influencer, if you like.

Here is how my favourite rant of all time started: *If you want my best advice, close your LinkedIn account today!* Harsh words, but it was the best advice I could give. After that attention-grabbing start, I shared the backstory.

Someone contacted me asking for my advice on how to use LinkedIn to reach out and sell to as many people as possible. He started the conversation by saying, 'I don't want to spend all day on LinkedIn connecting with people. I don't have time to be writing articles or answering people's questions. And I don't want to have conversations with people off LinkedIn either.'

I responded by asking him, 'What exactly *do* you want?'

'I just want to be able to direct people to our landing pages,' he said, 'so that hopefully they will buy our courses.'

Hence my rather harsh advice to him to close his LinkedIn account. I continued my rant, venting my frustration about people who want to experience the benefits of LinkedIn without engaging in the process, but finished the post with this promotional offer:

It's not that difficult to generate plenty of business through LinkedIn, but there are some fundamental issues that you need to be aware of. If you would like some tips on best practice for LinkedIn marketing, reply in the comments. If you're in Australia, I'll send you a copy of my book The LinkedIn Playbook. *If you're outside Australia, I will send you the PDF version. There's no opt-in required, and no, I won't add you to any database. Consider it a New Year's gift with no strings attached.*

This post gained a lot of attention. My rant resonated with many who responded with their own similar frustrations, the offer at the end led to great discussions in the comments about LinkedIn marketing tips, and the promotional offer left readers of the rant feeling pretty positive.

Step 3: The content mix

Hopefully, by now you have some great content ideas, and an understanding of the right type of content. Here's my thirteen-point plan as to how your content should be broken up over any given month. It's entirely up to you what will be in video form or text-based content.

- Interesting: Seven in total per month that are interesting enough for your community to want to engage and get in on the conversation. As this will represent over half of your monthly content, it makes sense, I hope, to mix it up between video, text only, and text with image.
- Your industry: Two per month that are specific to your industry, following the previously described format and spread a couple of weeks apart.
- Promotional: Two per month, and it's up to you to decide whether they should be spread over the month or close

together. Which option is better will depend on your strategy.

- Curated: One per month, share someone else's content. However, if you're struggling to come up with something from each of the other four options, by all means add an extra one of these until you can build up to the full thirteen pieces of content per month.
- Rant: One per month is always the maximum. As with the curated option, feel free to reduce this to every second month if you're more comfortable with that, especially in the early stages of your content creation.

Again, let me be clear here. This is what I personally consider an ideal mix and amount of content. If you're new to content creation and this seems a daunting task, start with a much lower number. Many people choose to start with four items of content per month in the first month, and build upwards until they reach full speed and are confident that they can be consistent.

I suggest it's better to start low and build than go up and down each month. Your community will get used to your level of content delivery, and consistency beats erratic behaviour every time.

Step 4: The content schedule

Based on the thirteen-point content plan, and being at this level consistently, you should aim to post every Monday, Wednesday and Friday.

If your clients and community are all over the world, like mine, it could be more challenging to have a specific time that is best to post. I always err on the side of simplicity. I believe that consistency is the key to long-term success. If your content follows the above process and is relevant to your microniche, the right people will gravitate to you and your content regardless of the time zone. LinkedIn's algorithms also work in your favour once they work out who your content best serves and is more likely to keep feeding it to them regardless of location or time.

We've now covered, in depth, the three pillars of the *like* phase. I'm sure it's obvious that the three stages—*know, like, trust*—are designed to build on each other, and each takes a bit more buy-in from your followers.

Getting known will be easy if you follow the process and the three pillars. Getting liked will take some work, but it's well worth the process. Creating trust is the step that will bring it all home seamlessly and is the main driver of effortless sales. The steps must follow each other in a logical sequence, however, to be effective. Take all the time you need in the *like* phase before moving onto *trust*. And then when you're ready, move onto the next section.

Karen Chaston

Karen is a Beyond Loss expert. Her retreats and programs (delivered physically and virtually) demonstrate the correlations between loss and all areas of your life. When individuals embrace these concepts, they easily move beyond any kind of loss and create a better everyday life. When companies embrace these concepts, they unlock the people and profits connection. Her motto is 'Life is too short to be suffering from any kind of loss. Unwrap the gift this has brought and then design a life that you live and love.'

What was the biggest challenge you were having with LinkedIn before working with the Prominence Global team?
To be honest, I was a little lost and haphazard in how to utilise LinkedIn as a way to get myself and my services out there. My lack of engagement, both in my content and growing ideal connections, was very disheartening. The time I was spending on LinkedIn was increasing with minimal ROI.

How has your time spent on LinkedIn changed since joining the program?
Through following the strategies provided, my LinkedIn profile has become first class. I love the thirteen posts per month strategy. It has provided the clarity and direction I was lacking. I am now spending less

time on LinkedIn with better results. The quality of my connections has improved and my connections are interested in genuine conversations which have led to some great collaborations and partnerships.

Can you share one or two benefits you have experienced since joining the program?

Each day I am connecting with new people and having conversations with my connections. I love the interaction and many collaborations that have been formed because of this strategy. People now know who I am, what I am passionate about and how I can assist them.

I have formed many friendships and collaborations within the program. Through engaging with other members' content, this is a natural progression. And best of all, it guides you to up the level of quality of your content.

I now have a detailed strategy plan for my content. I've created a rolling six-week plan for all my content, which is also repurposed to my website and other social platforms. I utilise and love all the different formats: text-based status post, status post with an image, a native video uploaded with transcript, and polls. I've even had success with events.

How has this impacted you, either personally or as results for your business?

My content engagement has increased from fifty views to over 3,000 and best of all I have people reaching out to know more about how I can help them to move beyond any one of the forty plus loss events that can affect all of our lives.

The program has resulted in me reaching more people. I want everyone to know that life is too short to be spending your time grieving and suffering. With a little guidance and a new perspective, you can move beyond any kind of loss and create your better everyday life.

For that I am very grateful to Adam and his amazing team.

Karen Chaston
www.linkedin.com/in/empowerwomen
www.linkedin.com/company/live-love-by-design
www.karenchaston.com

CHAPTER 13

Community and How to Build Yours

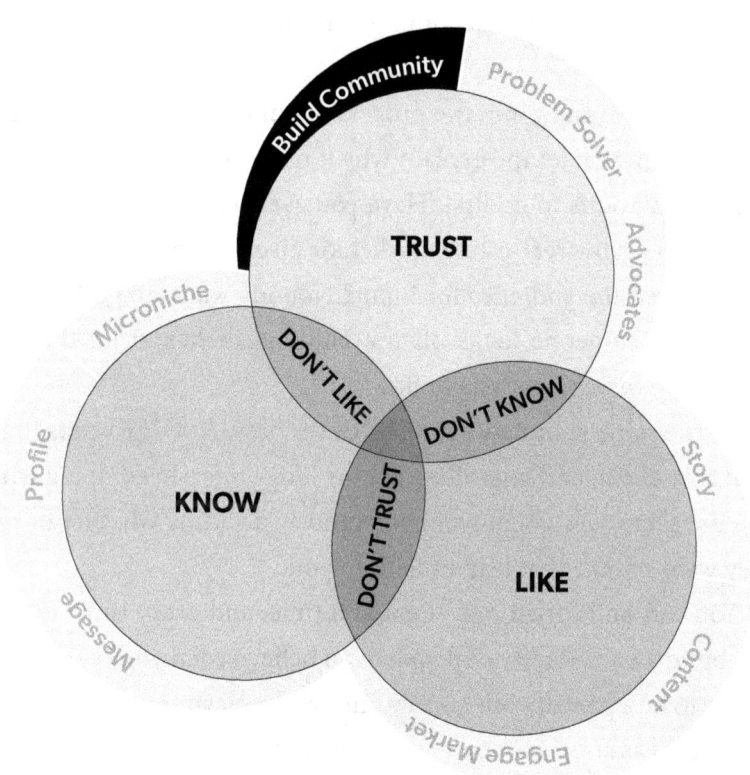

Let me ask you a question. When was the last time you made a significant purchase from someone you didn't trust? Unless you're selling Lamborghinis for $1,995 (and even then, most people would think twice), if people don't trust you, it's a hard slog to turn them into clients.

Creating that trust is a much easier road if people already know who you are, have a clear understanding of what you do, and they like you. And as I have outlined, there are three accelerators of trust: building a community, becoming a problem solver, and creating advocates.

So, let's dive right into the process of building a community, but before we do that let me explain why it matters.

Nobody wants to go first. Have you ever been to an auction for a house in a slow real-estate market, or given a presentation where you've asked the audience for input? Nobody wants to go first. But as soon as someone kicks off the bidding, or has given the first response, everything starts to flow.

It's the same with new products or services. Nobody wants to be your first client, and regardless of how long you've been doing what you do, every new client will be nervously deciding whether or not they want to take that leap of faith in you.

You can build trust one client at a time, and every time, or you can build a community of people who believe what you believe, are happy to be a part of your community, and sing your praises. People will feel reassured to know you have a community in place, and they can see a constant stream of activity from and to you, and an engaged tribe of people who seem to be just like them, by which I mean that they are interested in you, your expertise, and in working with you.

Community = Trust

Once people know you have your own community, trust will be established in most cases *before* you get to the sales conversation instead of it *being* the sales conversation. Think back over any recent interactions you've had that didn't end up with that person getting to the sales-conversation step. To those people actively looking for someone to solve their particular problem, you are a potential candidate. Maybe they've been to your website, and they've been following you for a while on LinkedIn and are seeing your content regularly.

When someone takes the first step from being a content consumer to being a potential client, the most important hurdle for them to overcome is finding out if they can trust you to solve their problem. This is where the conversation starts. If you cannot convince them of your trustworthiness, the conversation will go no further. They will go looking for alternatives, someone else to talk to.

Now imagine if they could become immersed in your community of like-minded people. That conversation would be much more likely to be about your service rather than whether you're the right person for them. As the leader of the community, your ability to influence and be seen as an influencer will be exponentially higher than if you simply remain the content creator who other people use to establish influence.

Having a great book on a subject or creating regular high-quality content will lift you above the masses in influence; having your own community will up your game every time.

Meet-ups

Every community needs a home, a place to gather and share their thoughts, ask their questions, and interact with each other.

If your clients tend to be localised in the same region, you might want to meet regularly with your tribe, face-to-face. You can use the Meetup website[17] as the home of your new community. You can use this functional site to set up your own group within minutes. Given that millions of people across the globe know, like and trust the website Meetup, it would be my platform of choice to use.

The real magic, though, happens through the live format of your group. There is simply no better way to build a community than having the ability to meet face-to-face on a regular basis. It allows your tribe to bring their colleagues and friends along, too, multiplying your community for you.

However, in most cases your community is best built online. No matter which online platform you choose, your group's objective should be clear and there should be rules to abide by. Make sure both of these are clearly stated and followed by you and your community members. There are three options to choose from.

---

17 www.meetup.com

1. **LinkedIn group.** While it is an option and may seem the logical choice, LinkedIn groups have long been plagued with challenges. LinkedIn has made a couple of attempts to revive them, but they still struggle in my opinion. However, there are exceptions to every rule and there is a small minority of LinkedIn groups that do very well. All I can suggest is if you choose to build your community here, moderate it well and keep control of the members' posting habits.

2. **Facebook group.** Facebook, in my opinion, does groups better than any other online platform. This is where ours is located and you are very welcome to join us at www.facebook.com/groups/LinkedIn2Success.

   Given that our group is 100 percent about LinkedIn, it might seem a little odd that I have created the group on Facebook. If any group should be on LinkedIn, mine would fit that bill. I have two specific reasons for using Facebook.

   The first is to spread risk. A reality we should all be mindful of is that we do not own any of our online profiles; most of us simply have rent-free access, and in some cases not even that. LinkedIn owns your LinkedIn profile, Facebook owns your Facebook profile, and the same can be said for every other social media platform in existence today.

   These organisations all change their rules regularly. I could share stories with you of businesses I know of that built their entire marketing ecosystem around both LinkedIn and Facebook, only to have their accounts closed on them for seemingly minor infringements of the rules. So I choose not to have all of my eggs in the one LinkedIn basket.

My second reason for using Facebook is that, as already stated, I believe Facebook groups are far superior to LinkedIn groups with regard to user friendliness.

3. **Membership site.** There is no shortage of options when it comes to platforms you can use to custom-build your own community site. These include WordPress, Ontraport, and MemberPress, to name just a few. Building your own platform will require a lot more time to set up, and there will likely be an associated cost as well. One of these websites will, however, give you the ability to design things exactly the way you want them to be.

It doesn't matter where you build your community, only that you have one and that you are the founder of it. Once you've established your community, it should be accessible from your LinkedIn profile. I also suggest that you create a position description that outlines what your group is all about, with a link to the group—this is one of those game-changing tactics that will make you stand out above the pack.

I should point out not all of your clients will want to be a member of your online community. Some will prefer to keep to themselves and just want you as their chosen service provider. They will still be swayed by your influence as the founder, however, so it's essential that they can easily see that your group exists. So make it obvious on your profile, and give it its own position description.

Having your own group is impressive in itself, but it's what you do with your group that makes all the difference. The majority of groups I see don't create influence for their founders. Rather, they are ghost towns of sorts. They may have impressive follower counts, but if nobody is active in the group, it's doing more harm than good.

Of course, the most active person in your group should be you. If you're not visiting your group daily, or at least Monday to Friday, as well as creating conversations and nurturing your community, you will miss the biggest value proposition your group offers.

There is a plethora of groups that attempt to create a real sense of community but follow a tired methodology of having themed days: Mentor Monday, Wednesday Wins, Friday Funnies and the like. These groups are at least trying to be engaging, but in my opinion these strategies fall short because they rely on the community to be posting and engaging.

A better strategy for you is to be the one posting and starting the conversations. There is nothing wrong with following a set routine that your group members get used to.

Q&A sessions

One of the best ways to generate high engagement is to hold regular Q&A sessions where your group members can send in questions about your chosen area of expertise. In answering them, you have a great opportunity to expand beyond your microniche and showcase your wider expertise, if that is appropriate for you.

These Q&A sessions can be done in two different ways. The first option is to simply pose the question yourself. An example from our group is where I might pose a question like: *Would you prefer your LinkedIn profile to generate leads or position you as credible?*

The second option is to hold a live Q&A session. If you're using Facebook, you can do this through Facebook Live, which is only visible to your members. Or you can invite your members to a live webinar that you run regularly. I like Zoom as a webinar platform, but there are plenty of other good options, too. You can then answer the questions your community has and upload the recorded session for those who couldn't make the live session to watch later if they choose to.

Managing your group

The number of your followers is not the most important factor, but you should be actively looking to grow your group. One of the best ways to do this is to invite your new and existing LinkedIn connections to come and see what it's all about, provided the people you invite would be likely to gain some value from being a part of your community.

I suggest you have two strategies for this step. The first is simply to go through your current connections and make a list of those you believe would benefit from membership. Give them a bit of an outline of what they should expect from their free membership and invite them to join.

The second option is to invite all of your new connections going forward, regardless of whether they request to connect with you or vice versa. Be proactive. Inviting them to check it out after you have connected is a great way to start a conversation, and it will also provide free value without making you look pushy.

I suggest that you don't start your group before the previous six accelerators we have covered are underway. What comes first is having a great profile, and a clear message about what your superpower is, and honing that down to your microniche. Give people the opportunity to decide they like you through your stories, by seeing that you're responsive to their engagement, and of course by creating that amazing content. This is important to get underway because people who know and like you are far more likely to want to join your community.

My final piece of advice before we move onto the next accelerators is to ensure that you have the administrator rights to moderate your community's ability to post to your group. Allowing off-topic content to roam inside your group will only annoy your members, especially if, as it often does, it revolves around members pitching their services to your members.

All good platforms will give you the option to moderate posts before they are visible to your members. If you have a repeat offender, you can privately message them and politely remind them of your objectives and rules. If they continue, then it's time to remove them altogether.

'Where there is not community; trust, respect, and ethical behaviour are difficult for the young to learn and for the old to maintain.' —**Robert K. Greenleaf**

Sean Hall

TEDx speaker, awarded innovator, and mental-health advocate Sean Hall has built his career on being an energising force of change for individuals, teams and brands. And it all started as a lycra-clad aerobics instructor in New Zealand.

Over the course of two decades of leadership in both customer and employee experience, Sean has five world firsts in bringing tech innovations to life, run a $10 billion telecommunications brand impacting 16 million customers, and designed culture strategy and strategic transformation programs for 40,000 employees. He has built two start-ups and been employee #11 in another.

But perhaps most importantly, Sean learned why wellbeing is important the hard way by suffering burnout, or what he calls an energy crisis, twice in three years.

As chief energist of human performance company Energx, he works with global brands like Facebook, Unilever, Deloitte, Google, Intuit, Contiki and AON who believe their most valuable assets are the collective energy and creativity of their people.

What was the biggest challenge you were having with LinkedIn before working with the Prominence Global team?
Getting 'seen' in a way that demonstrated the strategic value Energx brings to our clients. And then having those people see that human

performance is actually a strategic competitive advantage that is attainable.

How has your time spent on LinkedIn changed since joining the program?

I'd say it is more focused and therefore more effective. I have focused more on adding and providing value in the way I communicate versus promoting.

Can you share one or two benefits you have experienced since joining the program?

An increase of over 3,500 high-quality connections/followers in nine months. Energx and myself personally are increasingly being seen as differentiated from other wellbeing offerings in the market. We are the only ones demonstrating the link between mental wellbeing, productivity, innovation and inclusion in a data-driven way.

How has this impacted you, either personally or as results for your business?

I am confident we are on the right track in terms of building our brand presence and distinctiveness. We are now starting to average 2,500 plus views per post.

Sean Hall
www.linkedin.com/in/seanhall-competitive-advantage-productivity-burnout-creativity-energy-mental-health-wellbeing
www.linkedin.com/company/energx
www.energx.com.au

CHAPTER 14

Problem Solving

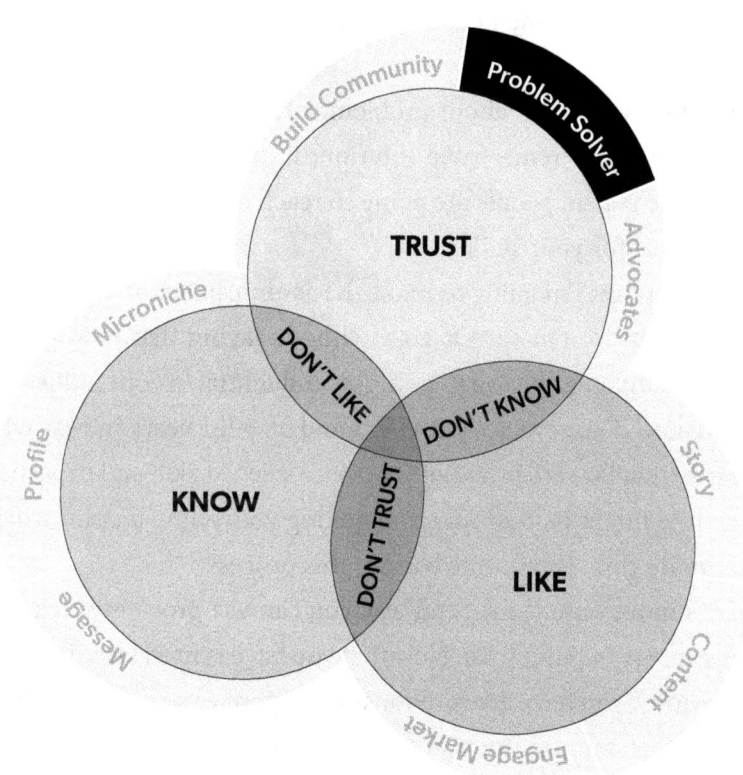

Everyone has a problem they need solved, and everyone loves the person who can solve it for them. Being very clear about the problem you solve is the fundamental backbone of your reason for becoming an influencer in your industry. It's the thing you are known for. As we covered in earlier chapters, it should be clearly outlined in your summary and your message to market.

There are two very important ways to go about problem solving in the influencer framework. There are also a couple of problems I see constantly with the next step, so I will cover those for you here, too.

The first way to go about problem solving is of course through your unique and remarkable solution; it's your expertise in what you do, the reason people are going to reach out to you and pay you handsomely for your skill.

At this point I'm going to make the assumption that you're great at what you do. I'm sure it goes without saying that it would be extremely difficult for you to be highly influential in your industry if you are not. If you cannot put your hand on your heart and say with integrity that you are proud of your hard-earned skill and expertise, your time might be best spent on getting yourself to a point where you *can* do this. Then come back to this process.

Let's move onto the second way you can use problem solving in your strategy to build trust. Now that you have started building your community, you have a forum for sharing your expertise to add real value to that community. You should invite your tribe to share their questions in your community that you will provide solutions for.

I can hear that question forming in your mind right now: *If I share all of my expertise for free, why would anyone need to pay me for my advice?*

I've lost count of how many times I have had this conversation. Let me assure you that the more you share your expertise, the more trust you will create and the more trust your community will have in you, beyond the enquiries you will have for your paid solutions. A lot of the content you share is going to solve problems for people. It's the reason they were attracted to you in the first place, and it will generate thousands of positive comments into the future.

The next chapter will cover this in detail, but let me just mention it quickly here. You will only have achieved influencer status when other people say you have, not when *you* do. Here's a comment left on one of my recent posts: *Your tips are priceless, Adam Houlahan ... other LinkedIn 'experts' can only eat your dust.*

Another person connected with me in this same post to find out more about our services and she is now a client. When we first spoke together on a Zoom call, she shared with me her reason for contacting me. She had been looking for someone on LinkedIn to speak to about lead generation and came across a video of mine in her feed. She looked at my profile, and all the recommendations from people I have worked with. She then spent a couple of hours going over all of my recent posts, and became convinced that I was the person she needed to speak to for help in generating more leads on LinkedIn.

Every week you will see tips from me about leveraging LinkedIn effectively. Every week I receive requests for interviews to speak at events or on podcasts to further share my expertise, and of course messages from people requesting conversations about how we could work together.

Using your community as a platform for problem solving is the fastest way to start creating the advocates you need to bring this process home (more about that in the next chapter).

Also, you can and should utilise other groups to share your expertise. LinkedIn allows you to be a member of up to 100 groups. Find a select few that have a reasonable following and are likely to have a number of your ideal client avatars as members. Where you can, share your knowledge when the right questions are asked, and where appropriate you will get the opportunity to invite these people to join your community to access more direct assistance. The more you are seen as the problem solver in these groups, and on LinkedIn in general, the more trust you create.

Note that I previously suggested LinkedIn groups may not be the best option to build your group, however leveraging someone else's group in an ethical way is still worth some of your time, as is commenting on people's posts outside of groups. I set aside time three or four days per week to simply search through my feed and make comments on other people's posts if I find them interesting. This also exposes your profile to a whole new potential audience. The more insightful you make your comments, the more likely people are to view your profile and reach out to you to connect for more information about what you do.

Your problems

As I alluded to earlier, there are two problems I see regularly that are created by increased influence. The whole point of the exercise is to create more opportunities to attract new clients and increase your annual revenue. However, if these flaws exist in your next steps, a lot of your existing, and soon to be increasing, conversations will not hit the mark. You risk becoming very busy attempting to find time to have your sales conversations, and very busy writing proposals. At first that might seem like the best problem to have, and, granted, in some ways it would be.

This book is about the process of getting you to the point of receiving these types of messages on a regular basis, but the real game changer is what happens once you do. To be honest, this section, which is the next step after becoming an influencer, could be an entire book in itself. That's not possible, but I'd feel like I had led you to the promised land and left you high and dry if I didn't cover this in at least a small amount of detail.

There are two ways that you can enjoy a higher conversion rate.

Once you have completed the influencer framework and have become that go-to person, your conversations will always be about the problem you solve. Every week I get messages on LinkedIn like this one: *An associate of mine recommended you in a Neil Patel paid mastermind group as someone who is really keyed-in on LinkedIn. I've got 16,000 connections but I don't monetise it well. I'd love to connect and learn from you.*

Or like this one: *I've been following your content here on LinkedIn for a while and just saw your latest video (nine-step formula on writing the ideal LinkedIn summary) and found it very interesting. I am keen to connect and understand how you can help me use LinkedIn more effectively.*

It's at this point that all the hard work could be undone very quickly and potentially tens of thousands, or even hundreds of thousands, of dollars lost.

My first suggestion is to make sure you have a booking scheduler that you can share with people to book in times to connect with you. I often see opportunities being lost that could so easily have been avoided through the use of this simple tool.

Let me share two scenarios using one of the above conversations.

Scenario #1: *Hi Jason, thanks for connecting and glad to hear you have found the videos, etc., useful. It would be my pleasure to touch base with you and discuss how we might be able to assist. When is a good time for you? Regards, Adam.*

This point is the beginning of an exhausting back-and-forward dialogue as I try to align Jason and my schedules to find a time to have a conversation. Most people check their LinkedIn accounts only once per day, twice if you're lucky, so by the time they have sent their message and you have seen it and responded, they will probably be gone for the day, as far as checking messages goes at least.

One of the shortcomings of the LinkedIn messaging system is the free messaging service. It's not an issue if you use Sales Navigator and understand how to track conversations with it, but the majority of people sending you a message will not have it, and may not be able to keep track of conversations even if they do.

The problem is that once someone reads your message there's no easy way for them to keep that message separate from the stream of incoming messages they receive afterwards, which means it's easily lost in the feed for both them and you. Out of sight out of mind, as the saying goes.

Often when we start working with new clients and looking at their recent activity, we see lost opportunities that have never resulted in a conversation. The message simply gets lost, and it's too hard to align two busy people's schedules.

Scenario #2: *Hi Jason, thanks for connecting and glad to hear you have found the videos, etc., useful. It would be my pleasure to touch base with you and discuss how we might be able to assist. Just select a day and time that suits you here [add link to booking scheduler], anything showing open works for me. You can choose whether you prefer a phone chat or a Zoom session, too. I look forward to connecting very soon. Regards, Adam.*

This scenario eliminates days of back-and-forward messaging trying to find a day and time to connect, and it also means that the conversation has moved off LinkedIn. If you don't hear back from your Jason within forty-eight hours, you will simply follow up again with the link. The program I use for this is OnceHub,[18] but two others are Calendly and Acuity Scheduling. Check them out and set one up as soon as you finish reading this chapter.

---

18 https://www.oncehub.com/

The second big-time drain eventuates once your meeting is booked and you're set to outline how you're going to solve your potential new client's problem when you connect. If, like the majority of your competitors, you offer a service, you will probably spend a large part of your sales conversations explaining what it is. Wherever possible, it's far better to have a product that is your service. Having to quote individually on every opportunity or having to explain what your service is and how it solves someone's problem is time consuming. Also, all your hard work could get you to this point and then end in confusion, or your potential new client needs time to think about it, or, even worse, your potential new client decides to shop your quote around other service providers.

Granted, it's not always possible to productise a service, but wherever possible you should do this. In most cases when I have spoken with clients about this and they believe they cannot productise, we've found ways that they can. Or at the very least we have created a range of products.

As an example, we have a DIY program, with Done With You and Done For You options. One hundred percent of the people we speak to fit into one of these two options, so the conversation is simply around which one will solve their problem best. The outcome is an efficient conversation, with almost no time spent on following up with time-consuming quotes or proposals.

In this scenario, the product information is always the same, as is the investment required, making it easy for someone who has already been through their journey of getting to know who you are, liking what you do, and having enough trust to reach out to you and make the decision to become a client.

Using a booking scheduler and having products will solve two big problems that you will face as a result of the increased interest you will create once you become highly influential.

> 'It's so much easier to suggest solutions when you don't know too much about the problem.' **—Malcolm Forbes**

Chandell Labbozzetta

Chandell is a confidence maker, a sales strategist and a master trainer of neuro-linguistic programming (NLP). Specialising in helping people fire their 'itty-bitty-shi*%y committee', she brings integrity back into the sales process for win-win-win outcomes.

Author of the book *Confident Closing—Sales Secrets That Grew A Business By 400 Percent in Six Months and How They Can Work For You*, she regularly trains individuals and companies around the world to increase their conversion. Chandell's purpose is to inspire confidence in others so that they can make empowered decisions.

What was the biggest challenge you were having with LinkedIn before working with the Prominence Global team?

The biggest challenge before working with Prominence Global was that we had loads of great content and no strategy to get that value in front of the right people. We had an inconsistent strategy and when we did hit the mark with a promotion/campaign, we often had 'vanity metrics' with Interest and Likes but no real substance or follow-up.

How has your time spent on LinkedIn changed since joining the program?

By following the Prominence Global strategy, we realised that investing time had direct rewards. Not only did visibility to the right audience increase, we noticed that we started to get enquiries from people who we were not connected to on LinkedIn directly but who had seen posts through second and third connections. It was incredible to hear that some of these people who wanted to do business with us had been following along without being connected for a couple of months.

Can you share one or two benefits you have experienced since joining the program?

There are so many … only a couple? Well, using the LinkedIn strategy helped me to really leverage my assets (book, presentations, blogs, videos, training, webinars). Instead of spending hours connecting 1:1 or to small groups, the net was easily cast wider to qualified, niche audiences. This has allowed us to run promotions with ease and more predictability. As we started to get traction with our strategy, I consistently received inbound (unsolicited) requests for meetings and proposals that led to large deals. I especially appreciated the education, feedback and advice about our strategy which enabled us to improve month on month.

How has this impacted you, either personally or as results for your business?

Being part of this program has created a great sense of confidence and certainty that my work is valued and appreciated on a larger scale. Most of all, it has given myself and my team a way to reach out to the people we really want to assist and provide value on a larger scale. Thank you to Adam Houlahan and the Prominence Global team.

Chandell Labbozzetta
www.linkedin.com/in/chandelllabbozzetta
www.linkedin.com/company/life-puzzle
www.lifepuzzle.com.au

CHAPTER 15

Creating Advocates

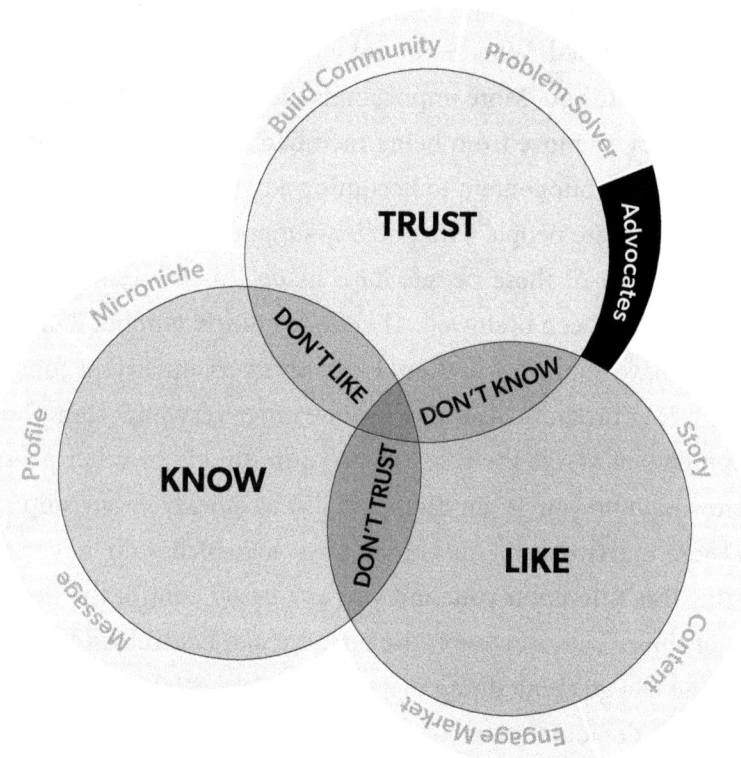

And so we arrive at the last of our nine accelerators of influence. In the previous chapter I mentioned an important concept, which I'll quickly repeat here: you will only have achieved influencer status when other people say you have, not when *you* say you have.

Social media is awash with self-proclaimed experts, influencers, thought leaders, gurus and game changers. This is the fake-it-till-you-make-it crowd; their egos are not backed up by their results. True influencers don't need to proclaim these titles; instead, they are bestowed upon them by their communities. The titles are earned not claimed. Whether or not you add this status to your title is entirely up to you. More important is the way you influence some of your tribe to move from being members of your community or consumers of your content to becoming advocates.

Advocates are people who publicly support or recommend you. When enough of these people have made this move, the title of influencer has been bestowed. There is no magic number denoting that you have made it; you should view this very important concept as a work in progress. And there is one other very important thing to remember. While the title can be yours simply by other people bestowing it on you, it can disappear just as quickly if they stop.

There are two very important ways in which your advocates bestow this title upon you, and you can easily control the flow of one of these. Let's start with the one you can control, and look at how you can go about doing that on a regular basis.

For a demonstration of this concept, scroll down to the Recommendations section in my profile: www.linkedin.com/in/adamhoulahan. You will see many that refer specifically to programs we run, and others from people who found enough value in the problem-solving content I regularly share that they were compelled to publicly state their beliefs.

LinkedIn recommendations

An important part of your strategy as you move forward should be to regularly entice people to give you a LinkedIn recommendation. You can even do this retrospectively by reaching out to current or former clients and colleagues you have worked with and simply ask them if they would mind doing you this honour. As long as you are both first-degree connections on LinkedIn, anyone can supply you with an official LinkedIn recommendation.

A WORD OF WARNING: Don't engage in the practice of swapping recommendations. Nothing on your journey to becoming an influencer is about being artificial; in fact, it's quite the opposite. Being an influencer is simply a framework you can follow to achieve your desired outcomes.

Many people who reach out to you on LinkedIn will not know you and will never have worked with you as a colleague or client. They might offer to give you a recommendation provided you return the favour. Be aware that the recommendations you receive and the ones you give, appear on your profile with links to the other people's profiles, showing the dates the recommendations were given. Nothing looks more contrived than every person who has given you a recommendation receiving one from you in return.

This is equally relevant with regard to people you do know and have worked with, so avoid asking your colleagues and clients to swap recommendations with you. Of course, there will be times when you will be quite justified in giving a recommendation to someone who has given you one, but make sure the recommendations are not done in close time proximity to each other.

Genuine recommendations

Here is my very simple four-point guide to receiving genuine recommendations:

1. Go through your cell-phone contacts or client files and make a list of people you have worked with as a colleague, or who were or are clients. From this list create a shortlist of people you believe you know well enough to have a conversation with about supplying you with a recommendation. They should be people you have had, or currently have, a good rapport with, or whom you know have achieved exceptional outcomes through your services.

2. Pick up the phone and give three of these people a call. Add a reminder in your schedule to do this every week going forward until you run out of people to talk to. I guarantee that if you select the right people, your strike rate will be exceptional if you have a conversation along the following lines first:

Hey, Kylie, Adam Houlahan here [polite conversation about family, work, weather, etc.]. *Kylie, there was actually a specific reason I wanted to reach out to you today. I'm putting some real effort into my LinkedIn profile at the moment and as part of that I need to get some recommendations. However, I want to be really authentic and make sure they are from people I have worked with in the past. I know you got great value from the work we did together. Would you be open to writing a few sentences in your own words about how I helped you?*

3. Let your new recommender know that you will send them a link on LinkedIn that will enable them to do this very easily. Almost everyone you have this conversation with will agree to do this for you, but most will be busy people just like you. Despite their good intentions, work and life could get in the way, so making it as easy as possible for them will improve the results dramatically.

   LinkedIn allows you to request recommendations, which you can do in three easy steps. First, on LinkedIn find the person you had your conversation with. Below their professional headline you will see the More tab. Click on this, and then click on Request a Recommendation.

   You now have the option to select both your relationship and your position at the time you and this other person worked together. You will see many options that should cover almost every scenario, so simply choose the most appropriate.

You can now add a short message to be sent with your request. By default, it will say something bland like, *Hi Kylie, can you write me a recommendation?* Delete the default message and create a more personal note referencing your recent phone conversation and then hit send.

Follow up by sending Kylie a text message or email to say that you have sent her your recommendation request, and ask her to check her messages on LinkedIn. Reiterate your appreciation for doing this for you.

4. As you move forward, you will find yourself working with more and more people, and you should still go through the above process with each one at the appropriate time. This shouldn't be at the beginning of your working relationship, and when you do it will depend on how your services work. If you have given a set task with a defined outcome or a result that you deliver, the appropriate time would be when you have delivered on your promise. If you work with people over a long timeframe or in an ongoing capacity, the right time will be up to your best judgement, but ideally it should be after a few months of working together, or when they have achieved a tangible outcome.

Content comments

As mentioned earlier, there is another equally important way for your advocates to bestow the honour of influencer on you;

however, it's less controllable than recommendations. This is via the comments on your content on LinkedIn and most importantly where your advocates choose to create their own content about you.

At first glance, it might seem that this is easily managed by simply asking people to do it in the same way that you ask for recommendations. But the type of content I'm referring to is not something you could easily ask someone for, at least not in my opinion. Instead, your advocates will create and share this type of content about you as a direct result of you focusing on providing great advice and being the problem solver.

Here are some examples of comments from my own clients:

- *I know and highly recommend Adam Houlahan as a LinkedIn expert trainer! I also just finished his latest book recently and recommend that as well. #business #linkedin*
- *Thanks for trying your best to work with very little #headshots #business #training #communication #fundraising #innovative #lifelonglearning #mentors Adam Houlahan #littlesteps*
- *Adam Houlahan and Michael (Mike) Clark sharing some sage LinkedIn wisdom here at WOTSO on the Gold Coast.*
- *Adam Houlahan is a social media expert who has had a fascinating career journey. As part of my #14InspiringLeaders podcast series, I've chosen Adam's interview out of 150 episodes to share as it'll provide inspiration to anyone considering entrepreneurship. Listen to his story, from his early childhood aspirations to join the Air Force, to creating a lifestyle business,*

becoming a waterski instructor to owning a chain of waterski businesses ... but how did he become the author of Secret Sauce and the sought-after social media strategist and expert he is today? You'll enjoy our conversation here: #podcasting #entrepreneurship #JaneCareerCoach #AdamHoulahan

- *How do you take time to enjoy life & learn? We work so hard & must recharge our batteries I ✈ over 10 hours to Budapest Hungary. When I have quiet time on the plane or early in the mornings is when I recharge and think about my goals & my life direction. Adam Houlahan's Play Book is my learning tool on the trip. I am joining 50 Entrepreneurs' Organization members & their spouses on an Avalon River Boat Cruise on the Danube River Avalon Waterways River Cruises #linkedingoals #enjoyment #Avalon #cruises*

Sharing of your content and commenting on your content will come from you: from your constant focus on creating exceptional content week after week (see chapter 12), and from you engaging with your community's comments (see chapter 10). This is how you can control the activity your advocates are undertaking.

This is not something that you need to control; the more organically and naturally it occurs the more power it will possess. Rest assured that this is where true influence lies. And here I'll repeat that little phrase for the last time: you will only have achieved influencer status when other people say you have, not when *you* do.

If I were to put a label on the process that is the nine-step guide to becoming highly influential in any industry, it would be *authority marketing.* Do your online searches and you will find no shortage of articles about this, and thought leadership or similar. It's mostly good content, and I not only agree with the concepts of authority marketing, but I have also lived by the principles for quite a few years now.

Is it the only form of marketing you should pursue? No, it isn't. Will it be the right methodology for every person who reads it? No, it will not. Is influence easy to obtain? I believe it is as easy as you choose to make it.

I've attempted to make this book similar to my earlier book, *The LinkedIn Playbook*; that is, I have written it as a playbook. It's designed to be a reference guide that you work your way through methodically, step-by-step, and come back to regularly over time. In this way you will get a sense of what you have achieved as you implement each step and cross it off your to-do list.

I have received many messages from people all over the world who have implemented the strategies from *The LinkedIn Playbook* and gone on to generate millions of dollars of combined revenue by following the outlined steps and adapting them to their individual circumstances. It is my hope that *Influencer* will sit on your desk, or within easy reach on your bookshelf, and that you'll refer to it regularly. Better still, keep both books together. *Influencer* does not supersede *The LinkedIn Playbook*, or in any way make this book redundant. It is a valuable resource in itself and should be considered an extension of the principles and action steps outlined in *The LinkedIn Playbook*. *The LinkedIn Playbook* was updated to keep it highly relevant in 2022. If you have the original version, I'd highly recommend getting the updated version.

> 'You don't need to change your message; you need to change your tribe' **—Suzette Vearnon**

Colin Hunt

Colin is a serial entrepreneur, mentor and business consultant with a keen interest in emerging trends. He is the founder of EzyAccounts, a franchise group that enables business owners to realise their potential in business, at home and in the community.

What was the biggest challenge you were having with LinkedIn before working with the Prominence Global team?
I had a LinkedIn account for several years but was not truly active. I remained skeptical about the justification for the time commitment.

How has your time spent on LinkedIn changed since joining the program?
After attending a workshop with Adam Houlahan, I recognised that the Prominence Global Academy program would enable me to leverage a strategic impact with a lower time commitment.

Can you share one or two benefits you have experienced since joining the program?
LinkedIn is now aligned with my purpose and business strategy. I am now confident in committing resources to LinkedIn because there is a well-structured plan of action. In addition, I'm able to respond promptly

to changes on the LinkedIn platform simply by following Adam's regular update sessions.

How has this impacted you, either personally or as results for your business?

Based on my experience, I'm now encouraging all of our franchisees to adopt a consistent LinkedIn presence supported by Prominence Global.

Colin Hunt

www.linkedin.com/in/colin-arthur-hunt

www.linkedin.com/company/ezygrowth

www.ezyaccounts.com

Becoming an Influencer

Using the Pyramid of Players concept to identify where you currently are, and where you want to be, is the first step in reaching your preferred position on that pyramid. Taking your time to work through each and every one of these accelerators and having a solid content strategy will help you reach that position, and you will go from being liked and known to being trusted, and with that combination, an influencer.

Even if you have been working on these areas for a while and feel you are doing well on your journey forward as an influencer, I recommend you still take some time to review where you are within each accelerator. Make a list of what you need to do as you read through this book, or go onto the Prominence Global website and download some of the resources and templates there. Our online programs are also aimed at assisting you to progress through the necessary steps for each of these pillars and their respective accelerators, and we regularly offer webinars and helpful sessions for people at all stages of the journey.

I wish you well and look forward to seeing your influence grow.

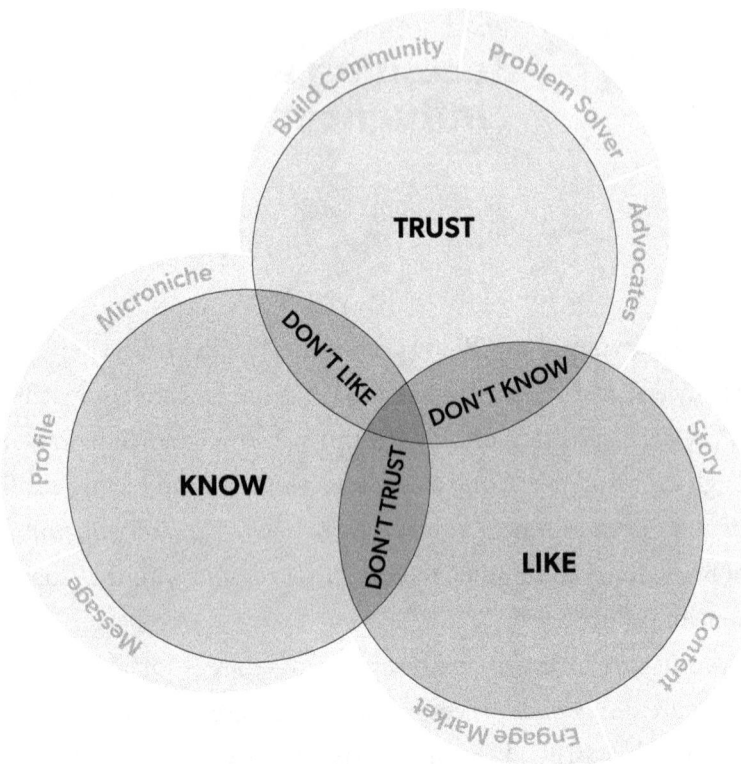

Ann Dettori Wilson

Ann is the founder of Dettori Publishing. She has been in the publishing industry for over a decade and is uniquely placed in working across traditional publishing and self-publishing.

Dettori Publishing encompasses three specialist companies: Post Pre-press Group, a typesetting company that produces books for major publishers and corporations including Pan Macmillan, Penguin Random House, Allen & Unwin, Magabla, Affirm and Carter Newell Lawyers; Independent Ink, a one-stop-shop for self-publishing authors such as Mia Freedman, Anton Tagliafero, and many others who want to bring their books to life; and Indie Experts, an independent publishing company helping non-fiction business authors in the before, during and after stages of writing and publishing.

Ann is also the best-selling author of The Entrepreneurs' Guide to Self-Publishing.

What was the biggest challenge you were having with LinkedIn before working with the Prominence Global team?

I was not sharing regular content and I did not appreciate how much of a negative impact this was having on building my authority and growing my connections. My profile was out of date and I was not utilising the many functions that LinkedIn offers.

How has your time spent on LinkedIn changed since joining the program?

I now post regularly and have a plan to create a variety of content. I enjoy connecting with people on LinkedIn and spend a lot more time building valuable relationships through messaging. I also have a clear message script that we send out to new connections and use to engage with existing ones.

Can you share one or two benefits you have experienced since joining the program?

My connections have increased dramatically and I have formed relationships with people around the globe, some of whom have become clients. The help I receive with the admin of connecting and messaging means I have a lot more time to focus on business growth and creating great content.

How has this impacted you, either personally or as results for your business?

Using the Prominence Global event format, we have held a variety of online events which have increased our database and had a positive impact on business. I have been able to continue building my personal brand and the business brand effectively.

Ann Dettori Wilson

www.linkedin.com/in/annwilson4

www.linkedin.com/company/dettori-publishing

dettoripublishing.com.au

Cathy Love

Cathy is the founding director of Nacre Consulting, which offers specialised business coaching for allied health professionals. Cathy and the Nacre Consulting team work remotely with all clients across several continents and time zones, leveraging technology to build relationships and connect with clients. Cathy is also an allied health business coach, speaker and author of the book *Becoming Chief: How to Lead Your Child's Special Needs Tribe.*

What was the biggest issue you had with using LinkedIn before you started working with Adam and Prominence Global?

Whilst we had sales navigator and a basic strategy in place, we hadn't stayed up to date with LinkedIn's ever-changing preferences and algorithms, and this meant that we were not getting the traction we wanted. We were also posting broad content that we shared across other platforms, so that really didn't get people thinking to the extent we wanted them to about taking the next steps, connecting with us and finding more about what we do and why we do it. Our entire set up and strategy needed a professional and skilled review to ensure we were best placed to leverage the powerful opportunities that LinkedIn provides.

What's changed for you since then?

Working with a team of LinkedIn specialists has provided us with a full review of why we want to use this platform. We now fully understand its role in our online presence, right down to the details we need to optimise for each page, as well as the scheduling and content strategy.

In what way has LinkedIn become a game changer for your business?

You don't know what you don't know. Working with a team of specialists fast tracks your knowledge and results from the LinkedIn platform.

What do you feel is the real value of using LinkedIn for your business, that puts it ahead of other forms of social media?

LinkedIn is a professional networking platform that helps us directly connect with allied health business owners by sharing practical content and leveraging the powerful functionality of sales navigator.

Cathy Love
www.linkedin.com/in/cathylove
www.linkedin.com/company/nacre-consulting
www.nacre.com.au

Bernie Landels

Bernie is an educator, speaker, practitioner, and the best-selling author of *Finding Their Feet: Every Parent's Guide to Milestones and Movement*, and as such came to LinkedIn only recently as part of her book launch strategy. Most of her contacts are within the health, parenting and education industries. Bernie read my books *Influencer* and *The LinkedIn Playbook* in 2021 and then got busy with building her own LinkedIn profile.

What was the biggest issue you had with using LinkedIn before you read Adam's books about LinkedIn?

I really didn't know how to leverage it as a professional platform, having only used social media for personal reasons previously.

What's changed for you since then?

It has opened my world—seriously. My connections have grown to many hundreds in a relatively short period of time, and I have nearly 1,000 followers on top of that. Positive working relationships have now been established. This has led to additional success with my book, and to new relationships with connections around the world. In addition, I can see other people in industries and groups of interest to me and engage with them easily as a highly credible influencer and specialist in my field.

In what way has LinkedIn become a game changer for your business?

The biggest thing that Adam taught me that others should know and do is that if you reach out to someone to establish a connection you should add a personal message; and if someone reaches out to you, again accept with a personal message. Equally, if people take the time to comment on your post, take time to respond. That's where the relationship and therefore business connectivity really takes on a new level of power.

What do you feel is the real value of using LinkedIn for your business, that puts it ahead of other forms of social media?

Being a professional platform for people to share their thoughts, news and views. Which for me results in expanding my own views and perspectives.

Bernie Landels

www.linkedin.com/in/bernielandels

www.bernielandels.com

Bronwyn Reid

Bronwyn is an international speaker, business person, and best-selling and multi-award-winning author. Her two books, *Small Company, Big Business* and *Small Company, Big Crisis*, are about business development and risk management, and she is a highly regarded influencer among SMEs in Australia and New Zealand. She was recently awarded as Thought Leader of the Year (Bronze) in the 2022 International Stevie Awards.

What was the biggest issue you had with using LinkedIn before you started working with Adam and Prominence Global?
Everything! Unless you have some guidance, posting on LinkedIn can be compared to shooting into the dark with a blunderbuss. You may get lucky and actually connect with someone you were aiming for, but there's a far greater chance that you won't. Like any business owner or manager, I did not have time (or money) to spare on a 'post and hope' strategy.

What's changed for you since then?
Steadily, I have built up my LinkedIn profile and following. At conferences and events, I have now been asked several times, 'Have I met you, or do I just know you from LinkedIn?'

In what way has LinkedIn become a game changer for your business?

Consistency. High-quality, consistent content. There is no short-cut recipe for LinkedIn success. What Adam and his team have added for me is the strategy behind using LinkedIn consistently, and making the best use of all the LinkedIn innovations that gives us more exposure.

What do you feel is the real value of using LinkedIn for your business, that puts it ahead of other forms of social media?

There certainly is a place for other social media platforms, but LinkedIn is definitely the 'professional' platform. Part of my audience is mid- to senior-level managers and executives of large organisations. They are the people who use LinkedIn—and the ones I need to be in front of. Other social media platforms do not really reach these people.

Bronwyn Reid

www.linkedin.com/in/bronwynreid

www.bronwynreid.com.au

My Gift to You

I do hope you enjoyed reading this book as much as I enjoyed the process of writing it, and not just the process of writing it, but also the thousands of hours of research, and the trial and error that went into validating the processes I have outlined before even putting pen to paper. Equally I enjoyed the process of updating it for you this year. More importantly, it's my hope that you will undertake your own journey to influence and reap the rewards I know await you. Please do share your journey with me; nothing excites me more than receiving those messages via email or on LinkedIn.

To find out how you can be in the top 1% of your industry take the LinkedIn Productivity Assessment: https://assessment.prominence.global/linkedin-productivity

You will also find more resources that support this book on my website: www.adamhoulahan.com.

The gift of giving

I consider it one of my greatest privileges to support so many charities through each of my books and the programs we have developed for entrepreneurs around the world. I'm proud to say that we have created over nine million impacts, or 'smiles' as we like to call them, at the time of completing this update in 2023.

By purchasing a copy of this book, you have helped provide an e-learning facility for a rural village. In fact, as a result of your purchase, eleven children gained access to the best learning environment available by introducing them to the latest technology for effective learning.

To meet the demands of today's global economy, it's crucial that all children receive quality education that equips them with twenty-first-century skills. Doing this together with you is a small yet important step in improving the lives of children who, without our support, would miss out on vital education.

I believe that real and meaningful change comes through the world's entrepreneurs; people just like you. My purpose is to help you create a powerful online presence that grows and accelerates your global footprint, so that together we can make a huge impact. You can access further information about the causes we support here: www.prominence.global/impact.

If you have read any of my previous books or been to my website, you know that I love quotes. Once again, I would like to leave you with one of my favourites:

'One of the best ways to influence people is to make them feel important. Most people enjoy those rare moments when others make them feel important. It is one of the deepest human desires.' **—Roy T. Bennett**

About Adam Houlahan

Adam understands the power of influence. You will regularly see him featured on a global list of events as a sought-after keynote speaker or being interviewed on podcasts. Over two thousand hours of research have gone into perfecting the process outlined in this book. The methodology outlined is currently being used by Adam's clients in multiple industries in Australia, New Zealand, North America, Singapore, Dubai, the United Kingdom, South Africa, Germany and the Netherlands.

For more information about Adam and Prominence Global, please visit his website or social media channels.

www.prominence.global
www.adamhoulahan.com

LI: www.linkedin.com/in/adamhoulahan/
TW: AdamHoulahan